George Boole's Lincoln, 1815-49

Editor: ANDREW WALKER

ISBN 978-0-9931263-5-2

Published by
The Survey of Lincoln, 2019

ACKNOWLEDGEMENTS

At the outset, I would like to thank all of the contributors to this collection. Their commitment and enthusiasm to the project has made my job as editor a very enjoyable one.

I owe a particularly great debt of gratitude to a number of the authors for the significant work they undertook helping me prepare the text for publication. Thanks particularly to Beryl George, Michael J. Jones, Dave Kenyon, Susan Payne and Geoff Tann.

I would also like to thank Professor Heather Hughes of the University of Lincoln for initially suggesting that the Survey of Lincoln might like to focus upon the subject of George Boole and his connections with the city. Professor Hughes enabled contact to be made between The Survey of Lincoln and the Heslam Trust, which had commissioned a public sculpture in honour of George Boole. Thanks are also extended to the Heslam Trust for its support of this project and for allowing a number of images to be used within the volume. Particular gratitude is due to Peter Manton, who chairs the Trust, and also to Electric Egg – especially Steven Hatton – for allowing the Survey of Lincoln ready access to the images produced for the Trust. Acknowledgment must also be paid to the tremendous work of the sculptor Antony Dufort.

A number of historic images in the volume have been made available for publication by Lincolnshire County Council, to whom thanks are due. Many of the contemporary photographs of Lincoln have been produced largely by Adam O'Meara and Dave Prichard. I am very grateful to them for these images.

The staff at Lincolnshire Archives, the Usher Gallery and Lincoln Central Library are also thanked for the assistance they have provided to the authors during the research for this volume. I would also like to acknowledge the considerable work over an extended period of time undertaken by Professor Desmond MacHale of the University of Cork in ensuring that George Boole's life is appropriately honoured. Many chapters in this volume have been informed by Professor MacHale's biography, *The Life and Work of George Boole: A Prelude to the Digital Age*, first published in 1985.

The Survey of Lincoln is grateful for the continuing support of the City of Lincoln Council. Finally, particular thanks are due to the University of Lincoln Library for its generous financial contribution that has assisted the publication of this volume.

Andrew Walker

INTRODUCTION

This third volume in The Survey of Lincoln's thematic-based series of publications takes a rather different approach from earlier titles. It focuses upon one notable nineteenth-century Lincoln inhabitant, George Boole, who was much associated with Lincoln from his birth in 1815 until he left to become inaugural Professor in Mathematics at Queen's College, Cork in 1849, where he worked until his relatively early death in 1864. This edited collection both locates Boole within his social and cultural networks in the city, and also explores some of Lincoln's prominent buildings and structures with which he would have been familiar.

George Boole today is much-heralded internationally as the 'grandfather of the digital age'. His basic logic and its significance are outlined in Malcolm Smith's chapter in the current volume. A timeline outlining key moments in Boole's life has been compiled by Susan Payne and is included in the volume. George was born into modest circumstances. His father, John, was a shoemaker, and his mother, Mary Anne, a former lady's maid. He spent the early part of his life living in the centre of Lincoln, with much of his childhood based in homes in Silver Street. Beryl George examines the evidence relating to the likely birthplace of George Boole in her first contribution to the volume.

George Boole soon proved himself to be both highly intelligent and industrious, displaying a great talent for languages and, latterly, mathematics. In 1830, his verse translation of the classical Greek poem 'Ode to Spring' was published in the *Lincoln Herald* newspaper when he was just 14 years of age. In 1831, he became an assistant teacher at a school in Doncaster, and then, in 1833, for six months he taught in Liverpool at the school of William Marrat, a Lincolnshire surveyor and publisher as well as teacher of mathematics. Later in 1833, George Boole returned to the Lincoln neighbourhood where he took up a position as assistant teacher at Robert Hall's academy in Waddington, before, in 1835, opening his own academy in Free School Lane, Lincoln. He returned to Waddington in 1837 to take up the position of head teacher at the school formerly run by Robert Hall. Then, in 1840, he opened a boarding school at 3 Pottergate in Lincoln. Alongside his school teaching, George Boole undertook a substantial amount of mathematical research, leading to the publication of some 30 scholarly articles between 1840 and 1848, many of which focused upon aspects of calculus. Rob Wheeler's two chapters in the volume plot Boole's time as a school teacher in Waddington and at Pottergate.

During his time in Lincoln, George Boole played an active role in the newly-opened Mechanics' Institute, based in Greyfriars, of which his father John had been a founding committee member, curator and librarian. George gave his first public address at the Institute in 1835. Lesley Clarke's chapter examines the Institute and George's involvement with this important educational and cultural organisation.

Like many relatively large British urban centres in the first part of the nineteenth century, th development of a significant middle class in Lincoln enabled the creation of a number of club associations and societies, which facilitated the social and cultural interaction of the Lincoln professional adult male population. Assembly rooms, reading rooms and libraries became the venue in which much of this self-improvement and social and cultural exchange took place. George Bool played an active part in this social milieu, as is made clear in the chapter entitled 'Accommodatin a thirst for knowledge in George Boole's Lincoln'. Amongst the reading material made available to members of Lincoln's libraries and reading rooms was a growing range of local newspaper titles Some of these were rather short-lived, but others became established and reputable sources o valuable local intelligence, to which George occasionally contributed and whose activities were regularly reported. Andrew Jackson's chapter highlights the key developments in the growth of the Lincolnshire press during the first half of the nineteenth century.

George Boole was involved in a number of societies and associations with education as their principal focus. In addition to the Mechanics' Institute he was also very active in the newly-established, but short-lived, Lincolnshire Topographical Society, to which he delivered a number of lectures. He also played a part in the Early Closing Association, which, in 1847, brought about through its campaigning a ten-hour day in the city for all shop assistants, apprentices and other workers. In celebration of the movement's success, Boole delivered an address entitled 'The Right Use of Leisure'. In the same year, he also became a founder and trustee of the Lincoln and Lincolnshire Penitent Females' Home. Although throughout his engagement with social and cultural life within the city, George Boole sought to engage across the party political divide, his path did cross with that of Thomas Cooper, the active Chartist. Richard Skipworth's chapter plots the relationship between the two men. George Boole's commitment to facilitating improvement in others also led to his involvement with the Benefit Building Society, a topic examined by Geoff Tann.

Boole's time in the city of Lincoln coincided with considerable physical changes to the townscape, some of which had very significant impacts upon the life of the city's inhabitants. These form the focus of a number of chapters within the volume. During the 1840s, as Adam Cartwright examines, the arrival of the railway in the city had considerable economic, social and practical consequences for Lincoln's inhabitants. The coming of the Midland and Great Northern railways, and their associated stations in 1846 and 1848 respectively, enabled significantly speedier journeys to be made across the country to and from the city – though, thanks to the new level crossings, not within it – and hastened the flow of information, which certainly assisted Boole in his academic work and networking. Beryl George's two chapters on the Corn Exchange and developments in the High street and Guildhall Street make clear the considerable escalation of the commercial life of the city during the later part of Boole's life in Lincoln.

Other significant physical developments within the city during Boole's time included the construction of a number of substantial new places of worship, perhaps most notably the Wesleyan Methodist Chapel (known colloquially as 'Big Wesley') on Clasketgate, opened in 1836. This replaced an orchard, familiar to George Boole during his childhood. Designed by W.A. Nicholson, whom Boole knew, the building comprised a place of worship, a vestry and school rooms, accommodating a congregation of well over 1000. Michael J. Jones's chapter considers how the considerable construction work in the city during the 1840s brought about encounters with the past as significant archaeological finds were made, for instance during the building of the railway level crossings, the Great Northern Railway station and the extension of the prison within Lincoln castle. As the chapter makes clear, national interest was aroused in these discoveries and led to the annual conference of the recently-founded Archaeological Institute of Great Britain and Ireland taking place in the city in 1848. Amongst the papers read at the conference was one written by George Boole.

In addition to the series of innovative mathematical papers produced by George Boole in Lincoln during the 1830s and 1840s, the city was also the location of some significant advances in mental health treatments at the Lawn Asylum, the extensive premises of which were opened on Union Road in 1820. These developments were overseen by Edward Parker Charlesworth and Robert Gardiner Hill, and are considered in a chapter produced by Rob Goemans and Nigel Horner.

The final section of the book focusses upon the memorialisation of George Boole within Lincoln. His early death at the age of 49 caused much sorrow and regret in the city. In late November 1864, Boole had walked three miles in heavy rain from his home to work in Cork, lectured in wet clothes and, subsequently, he became ill. He died on 8 December 1864 and the apparent cause, outlined in his obituary in *The Times* was 'an effusion upon the lungs'. He was survived by his wife of nine years, Mary Everest Boole, and five young daughters. The appreciation of Boole expressed by his contemporaries forms the focus of a chapter by Geoff Tann. A separate chapter examines the stained glass window produced in recognition of George Boole's achievements that was completed in 1866 and installed in Lincoln Cathedral in 1869. Susan Payne, archivist of the Rollett Collection, which contains a substantial collection of primary source materials relating to Boole, summarises the main content of the collection, for which there is not at present a readily accessible catalogue. A contribution is also included by Susan that examines the ways in which Lincoln marked the centenary of George Boole's death in 1964. This included the unveiling by his grandson of a plaque in his honour at 3 Pottergate, the site of his 'boarding school for young gentlemen'. More recent recognitions of George Boole's achievements and his connections with the city are also explored. Dave Kenyon's chapter focuses upon the High Street plaque unveiled in 2015 in honour of Boole's birth bicentennial, and outlines the author's central involvement with this memorial. The book's final chapter details some other recent memorials marking the significant contribution to scientific knowledge made by this long-time resident of Lincoln. It highlights some other aspects of the Boole birth bicentenary celebrations in the city, the opening of the Boole Technology Centre, and the commissioning of a high-profile sculpture. This work, by the internationally-renowned sculptor Antony Dufort and commissioned by the Heslam Trust, at last provides a substantial physical recognition of the mathematician's significance within the centre of his home city.

Andrew Walker
Rose Bruford College

Key dates in George Boole's life with particular reference to Lincoln

Susan Payne

1815.   2 November. Born in New Street, Lincoln (present-day 34 Silver Street), son of John and Mary Ann Boole, baptised on 3 November at St Swithin's Church, the site of which is west of the current church, on the opposite side of Free School Lane.

c.1816.   The Boole family moved to 49 Silver Street, Lincoln, (no longer standing) near to the church of St Peter at Arches which then stood opposite the Stonebow.

1817.   His sister, Mary Ann Boole, was born.

1819.   His brother, William John Boole, was born.

c.1819.   Pupil of Miss Clarke at house adjoining 49 Silver Street.

c.1820.   Pupil of Mr Gibson in Mint Lane, Lincoln.

1821.   His brother, Charles Boole, was born.

1822.   Pupil at the National School opposite his home in Silver Street, Lincoln.

1828.   Pupil at Mr Thomas Bainbridge's Classical and Commercial Academy on Fish Hill (now Michaelgate), Lincoln.

1830.   His verse translation from Greek of the poem, *Ode to the Spring*, was published in the *Lincoln Herald* newspaper.

1831.   Engaged as assistant teacher in Mr Heigham's School in South Parade, Doncaster

A tourist interpretation board, at the corner of Eastgate and Northgate, outlining George Boole's achievements. (*Adam O'Meara*).

1833.   For six months, George Boole taught at the school of William Marrat (1772-1852) in Liverpool and studied under him. (Marrat was personally known to Boole's father. He came from Sibsey, Lincolnshire and was a surveyor and publisher as well as a teacher of mathematics. Marrat published a map of Lincoln in 1817.)

1833.   Engaged as an assistant teacher at Mr Robert Hall's Academy in Waddington, near Lincoln.

1834.   Became a member of the new Lincoln Mechanics' Institute of which his father was a founding committee member, lecturer and the curator. The rest of the Boole family lived in part of the Greyfriars' building occupied by the Mechanics' Institute.

1835.   5 February. Delivered his first public address, which was at the Mechanics' Institute, on the occasion of the presentation of a marble bust of Sir Isaac Newton (which is now in store at The Collection, Lincoln). This became his first published paper.

1835.   Opened his own academy in Free School Lane, Lincoln where the Boole family also lived.

1837.   Became the head teacher at Waddington Academy, near Lincoln, leasing the school and house of the late Robert Hall, where the Boole family also lived.

1839.   First corresponded with Duncan Farquharson Gregory at Trinity College, Cambridge, who encouraged him to develop his ideas.

1840.   While at Waddington, his paper, *Researches on the Theory of Analytical Transformations*, was published in the new *Cambridge Mathematical Journal* edited by Duncan F Gregory.

1840.   Opened a 'boarding school for young gentlemen' at 3 Pottergate, Minster Yard, Lincoln, where the Boole family then lived.

Grave of John and Mary Boole, St Margaret's Churchyard, south east of Lincoln Cathedral. (*Adam O'Meara*).

Grave of John and Mary Boole, St Margaret's Churchyard, with Lincoln Cathedral in background. (*Adam O'Meara*).

1844. *On A General Method of Analysis* (1843) was published in *Philosophical Transactions of the Royal Society*.

1844. Was awarded the first Gold Medal of the Royal Society for mathematics.

1847. Was one of the founders and trustees of The Lincoln & Lincolnshire Penitent Females' Home established off Asylum (now Carline) Road, Lincoln.

1847. *The Mathematical Analysis of Logic* was published, his first work on symbolic logic.

1848. His paper *On The Philosophical Remains of Bishop Grossetête* was read on his behalf at the Fifth Annual Meeting of the Archaeological Institute of Great Britain and Ireland held in the County Assembly Rooms in Lincoln and other city venues.

1848. His father, John Boole, died at 3 Pottergate, Lincoln and was buried in the churchyard of St Margaret in the Close.

1849. A testimonial supper was held at *The White Hart Hotel*, Lincoln in honour of his appointment as the first Professor of Mathematics at Queen's College, Cork.

1854. *An Investigation of the Laws of Thought on Which are Founded the Mathematical Theories of Logic and Probabilities* was published.

1854. His mother, Mary Ann Boole, died at an address in New Road, Lincoln and was buried in the churchyard of St Margaret in the Close.

1855. 11 September. Married Mary Everest (1832-1916) at Wickwar, Gloucestershire.

1856. First daughter, Mary Ellen, was born.

9

1857.   *On the Comparison of Transcendents, with Certain Applications to the Theory of Definite Integrals* was published.

1857.   Was awarded the Keith Medal by the Royal Society of Edinburgh.

1857.   Was elected a Fellow of the Royal Society, London.

1858.   Second daughter, Margaret, was born.

1859.   *A Treatise on Differential Equations* was published.

1860.   *A Treatise on the Calculus of Finite Differences* was published.

1860.   Third daughter, Alicia (Alice), was born.

1862.   Fourth daughter, Lucy Everest, was born.

1864.   Fifth daughter, Ethel Lilian, was born.

1864.   8 December. Died at his home in Ballintemple, Cork and was buried in the churchyard of St Michael's Church of Ireland, Blackrock, County Cork.

THE SIGNIFICANCE OF GEORGE BOOLE'S WORK

Malcolm Smith

George Boole developed a process of logical thought which breaks down any complex problem into a sequence of simple steps based on the comparison of two statements as being either true or false. Boolean Logic states that we can compare statements of true and false at each step in the sequence to arrive at a result using only three fundamental choices for our decision. These options are called Boolean Functions:

1) If A is True AND B is True then the result is also True

2) If A is True OR B is True then the result is also True

3) The NOT function simply inverts the truth value of any statement. So, if A is True, then NOT A is False. Similarly, if A is False, then NOT A renders it True.

By breaking down our problem into this sequence of simple AND, OR, and NOT decisions we can arrive at a solution.

Boolean Logic is the foundation upon which all digital devices are built. Mobile phones, digital televisions, and all computers, from laptops to the most complex, contain millions of Boolean AND, OR, and NOT logic gates which compare inputs of a 0 or a 1 representing false or true. Modern digital devices can make the logical comparison billions of time each second. A computer programme or a phone application uses Boolean Logic to convert a problem into the very complex sequence of small steps and individual decisions of AND, OR, and NOT that the digital device hardware can then execute.

In the 1940s, Boolean Logic and electronic devices that implement the AND, OR, and NOT Boolean Functions became the foundations for the digital revolution. They are like bricks to a builder of houses – simple building blocks which can be stacked together to create astonishingly

A sculpture of George Boole, designed by Antony Dufort.
(Courtesy of the Heslam Trust and Electric Egg?

complex applications. In the early days of computing, devices were built with a few hundred blocks each of which could make a true or false decision in one thousandth of a second. These early devices were used to solve problems such as the routing of telephone calls. Today, mobile phones contain millions of Boolean Logic gates and they make AND, OR, and NOT decisions billions of times a second. These modern devices, though, are still using the same Boolean Logic as was applied 80 years ago. The difference is that there are now millions of Boolean gates crammed into a microprocessor chip that executes these Boolean Logic instructions.

The application programmes used today are written to convert whatever the application needs to do into the binary code the hardware understands. This coding creates the sequence of simple statements that Boolean Logic can execute. For a modern device it is impossible for a human programmer to write the code all the way down to the simple sequence of Boolean Logic. Computers and Boolean Logic are used to convert the programmer's high-level Source Code statements into the more and more detailed code understood by the logic within the device. With modern devices these programmes can be very large. The computers that control a Boeing 787 aircraft have about 12 million lines of programme source code. Facebook is reported to need 61 million lines of code.

Digital devices based on Boolean Logic are so successful and so useful because however complex a problem may be the data can be defined as a sequence of binary code – as a 0 or a 1 – and the decisions can be reduced to the simple AND, OR, and NOT logical comparison of the stream of 0's and 1's invented by George Boole. Each time screens are touched on mobile phones or keys tapped on laptops, thousands of Boolean Logic AND, OR, and NOT decisions are executed. As viewers watch television, the millions of pixels on the screen are being updated for colour and shade by a stream of Boolean Logic decisions.

Although Boole is justifiably remembered for his contribution to digital technology, this was not actually his life's work. His youthful passion was calculus. He published over 30 research papers on aspects of the field whilst he was still working as a schoolteacher in Lincoln. Some of these insights became absorbed into the general practice of calculus, which underpinned almost all twentieth-century scientific endeavour.

George Boole never made a fortune from his genius but he created the essential foundation for the modern digital world.

34 SILVER STREET, LINCOLN: GEORGE BOOLE'S BIRTHPLACE

Beryl George

It is generally stated that George Boole was born at number 34 Silver Street, Lincoln. There are two problems with this: Lincoln did not use street numbers in 1815 and George's baptism records his parents' address as 'New Street'. George's sister, Mary Ann, relates that he was born at 34 Silver Street, so one has to assume that she was correct: certainly concerning the numbering up to the point when she left Lincoln in 1854. But is that the same place as number 34 Silver Street today?

One of the confusions comes from the changing names for streets. From the 1790s until around 1820, the east end of Silver Street, connecting to the north end of Broadgate, was usually termed 'New Street' or even 'New Road' (although the latter usually referred to what is now Lindum Road).

Number 34 Silver Street is currently occupied by Starkey & Brown, Estate Agents. The taller part of the premises, on the right side, is the site where George Boole was born, and may be the actual house in which his birth took place. (*Geoff Tann*).

13

Precentorial lease, 25 June 1842. (Reproduced with permission of Lincolnshire Archives, Lincolnshire County Council. CC107-108941).

There are newspaper references to] Boole, boot- and shoe-maker from July 1809, when he is described a working in New Street. In 1812 Boole was in New Road, but in 181? he had moved to new premises in 'the New Street', adjoining Mr C. Curtois's Cabinet and Upholstery Warehouse'.

Before street numbering in Lincoln was introduced in the late 1830s, by the Lighting and Paving Commission, reference was made to the previous or adjoining occupier to locate particular premises (a practice which continued in legal documents). Charles Curtois, cabinet maker and upholsterer, had gone into the trade with his aunt, Mary Curtois, following the death of her husband in 1802, but dissolved the partnership in 1812. Charles set up on his own in new premises in May 1813, advertising in the *Stamford Mercury* to this effect.

In June 1814, Charles Curtois formally took on the lease of this property from Rev. Dr John Pretyman, Precentor of Lincoln (the land having been part of the old Holy Trinity churchyard). The premises were described as:

> All that newly erected shop with the ware rooms over the same situate in the parish of St Swithin in the city of Lincoln aforesaid together with a newly erected messuage [house] adjoining to the same shop on the west in the occupation of John Boole with the yard at the back of the said messuage and shop with a workhouse thereupon built...

The 'shop and messuage' were abutting the New Street to the south, ran north to a 'common lane', had a garden on the west side, and a house occupied by George Rylatt on the east. So by 3 November

815, John and Mary Anne Boole were living in New Street, St Swithin's parish, when they baptised their son George. But where is that house now?

One way to track the property is through Charles Curtois. Unfortunately he did not survive very long, dying at the early age of 42 years in 1822, and his house and premises were subsequently put up for sale. The description of the premises for the auction in July 1822 included shop, showrooms, workshops and also a messuage or dwelling-house (with yard, garden and brewhouse adjoining) in the occupation of John Curtois, grocer (Charles' father). In the event, the workshop premises were let to Powell and Reynolds, who had worked for Charles Curtois.

Meanwhile, John Boole had already moved, with an advertisement in September 1822 giving him as one of the occupants of 'two handsome and spacious shops' near St Peter at Arches' church.

At the renewal of the lease of Curtois' premises in June 1828 (repeated attempts at sale by one of his executors, James Simpson, having failed), the properties were being occupied by James Reynolds, upholsterer and James Millsom, grocer. There remained a garden to the west of Millsom's house and shop, and the layout of the properties remained similar to 1814, although the lane to the north was now described as 'leading from Butchery Lane' (now Clasketgate). It was still described as in 'New Street', although Silver Street was now the usual description in newspaper advertisements.

Also in 1828, properties in the City of Lincoln were valued for the purposes of assessing them for payment of the new Lighting and Paving Rate. The two premises were listed with 'Trustees of the late Chas. Curtois' as proprietor. James Reynolds occupied an 'upholsterer's shop, dwelling house, workshop, yard etc' at an annual value of £31, and F.A. Sayles occupied a 'house and small garden' valued at £22.

John Boole was shown in St Peter at Arches' parish in the 1828 valuation, where he was occupying a house, shop and yard next to the churchyard, the property of John Fish, valued at £30. This may indicate that the premises are slightly larger than where George was born, or it may relate to a more commercially advantageous position (nearer the High Street).

James Reynolds remained in Silver Street until 1834, when George Wilson took on his premises. He was also an upholsterer and cabinet-maker who was branching out into paper-hanging. By 1839, William Wallace (who ran a paper-hanging, upholstery and cabinet business) had moved in, with his premises described as nearly opposite Zion Chapel, which was on the south side of Silver Street and later replaced by a larger Methodist chapel (and now site of a car park). In Pigot & Co's directory of 1841, William Wallace is at number 33 Silver Street. A new precentorial lease, signed in 1842 by George Reynolds, shows Mr Hainworth, surgeon, next to Wallace in what can be established as number 34. This is confirmed in Hagar's 1849 directory.

In March 1856 the Lincoln Stamp Office moved into number 34 Silver Street with its Comptroller Arthur Trollope, living on the premises. The precentorial lease of October 1856 showed some alteration to the layout of the two premises, with both now running north to Clasketgate. The Lincoln Stamp Office remained there until 1878.

From this point the property was occupied as office premises, first by Swan Brothers & Bourn (solicitors) from 1878 to 1907 and then by Langley & Tweed (later Langley's, solicitors) from January 1908. The location of the property can be confirmed both by street number and, importantly, with references to plans.

Using a combination of leases, newspaper references, directories and plans, it is possible to confirm that the house where George Boole was born was, indeed, what is now number 34 Silver Street.

Robert Hall's Academy at Waddington

Bob Wheeler

Robert Hall's Academy at Waddington was taken over by George Boole from 1838. It was a relatively small school, accommodating male pupils. Some sense of life within such a school can be obtained from reading the work of Charles Dickens, most notably his work *David Copperfield*:

> A short walk brought us—I mean the Master and me—to Salem House, which was enclosed with a high brick wall, and looked very dull. Over a door in this wall was a board with SALEM HOUSE upon it; and through a grating in this door we were surveyed when we rang the bell by a surly face, which I found, on the door being opened, belonged to a stout man with a bull-neck, a wooden leg, overhanging temples, and his hair cut close all round his head.
>
> 'The new boy,' said the Master.

The early-Victorian school is so unfamiliar to most readers that it is worth approaching the subject through the medium of fiction. The Mr Creakle who ran Salem House School was a bully and a brute – Charles Dickens loved to accentuate characters – and there is no suggestion that Robert Hall was at all like him; but Dickens does not alter the *institutions* his characters inhabit. Let us therefore examine the institution through David Copperfield's eyes.

There are perhaps no more than twenty boys: they fit easily enough in a single classroom and share a common dormitory. Most of the teaching is done by the proprietor; he has a couple of teaching assistants, ill-paid and low in status. The domestic side is run by Mrs Creakle; and the high wall gives the place the air of a prison – although the boys do get taken to church on Sundays. How much of this was true of Robert Hall's Academy?

We know more about the assistants than almost anything else. Robert Coddington Moore left in 1819, at the age of 18, having been recruited by the new squire of Harmston to take on the charity school there. In 1828, a John Ross, schoolmaster, appears on the Militia Roll, aged 28; we may presume him to be another of Hall's assistants. In 1833, George Boole himself was recruited as an assistant. Although only 18 years old, this was his third teaching post. He left after a year to establish a day school in Lincoln. Finally, William Wright appears in the record in 1835, aged 22 years. He probably left in 1839, being appointed master of the Free School at Folkingham. This tends to suggest the assistants were, for the most part, capable young men establishing themselves in the teaching profession. They must have taken a significant share of the teaching.

By the time Boole arrived, Hall was aged 65, and he may have been shrinking the school. At the 1811 census the household had numbered 49; in 1821 it was down to 26, of whom 17 we probably pupils. In 1837 we know the names of 20 pupils, so perhaps the number had stabilise One problem with figures for total household size is that the establishment was a farm as well as school. The farming was undertaken by Hall's son John. By 1836 Hall was a widower, but he ha two daughters at home: perhaps they ran the household for him.

Schools like this tended to focus on modern subjects of evident utility. When George Boole issue a prospectus in 1839, he included book-keeping and surveying within the core syllabus; Latin an Greek were available at an extra charge, along with 'the higher mathematics'. That core syllabu probably continued the subjects that Robert Hall had offered. We certainly know that surveyin; played a significant part and there were 'folio books' that needed to be ruled and which arrived from and went back to, Lincoln. One wonders whether Hall was actually using the pupils to keep the books of certain Lincoln clients!

We know so much about the period 1835-7 because William Wright was enjoined by Hall to keep a diary. Wright was certainly dutiful, recording the weather each day as instructed, but his abilities as a diarist were limited. He tried to record what it was that made a day different, and that rarely concerned teaching, but rather the visit of the butcher, or of the man who came to cut the boys' hair. We are told the text for the morning and evening sermons at the parish church each Sunday. We are told almost every Sunday that 'Part of the Gentlemen went to the Lecture at night [the evening sermon] and part to Chapel.'

Surveying is mentioned frequently: in one week in April 1837, 'The Gentlemen went surveying' on four days and would have gone on a fifth but for the weather. In part, this is because Wright had a particular interest in surveying: he undertook a certain amount after his move to Folkingham. It also justifies a mention because it was a change from indoor teaching. It is usually difficult to establish the nature of the surveying, but we have occasional clues. A 'plan of Mr Hall's premises' was probably a survey of the buildings done with a tape-measure. Surveying 'some turnips for Mr John' perhaps implies surveying the area of a field, digging up a few turnips and calculating the weight of turnips per square yard. Taking an 'Eye-Draught' is a more specific term: sketching the detail without measuring it but possibly fitting it in within a skeleton survey that had been measured earlier. Waddington stands on the Cliff and there are numerous viewpoints from which an Eye-Draught could be taken.

Robert Hall's Academy, now Toynbee Court, Waddington.
(*Image courtesy of Andrew Thorne*)

Why was so much time spent on surveying? It provided healthy outdoor exercise. Certain aspects might be of use in later life. It necessitated sundry arithmetical calculations. Not least, making the finished plan developed skill in drawing and in lettering, both of which were regarded as useful accomplishments.

What about the pupils? Almost all were boarding; in October 1836 there was just one day boy. In some cases their homes were close: Master Hales was the son of a substantial farmer at Harmston, little more than a mile away. Boarding school was seen by the middle classes as a valuable stage in a boy's growing-up. And, so far as one can tell, the boys were indeed from middle-class families.

Was the Academy a happy place? It is difficult to judge from a single diary but there are indications that Hall tried to ensure a modicum of variety. His birthday was kept as a holiday and the boys were given plum cake and ale. In November 1835 a ventriloquist came and performed. When the Assizes came to Lincoln – always regarded as a great public spectacle – groups of boys were allowed to go to Lincoln to watch. On 26 October 1836 'during the afternoon there was a Squirrel come out of the fir-tree into the Yard. The Gentlemen caught it and killed it.' One envisages a noisy and joyful scrummage. There is no indication that Hall showed any disapproval, whereas at Salem House one feels the boys would have been too terrified to give chase.

David Copperfield laments that he learned nothing at Salem House. Robert Hall's pupils probably found their time more instructive. Master Hales was no doubt proud to show his father how he could estimate the weight of a crop of turnips. Master Simpson, who left to be apprenticed to a Gainsborough ironmonger, must have found his acquaintance with book-keeping useful, even if his new master kept his books on a somewhat different system. And all the boys would be able to write a respectable letter – perhaps somewhat stilted in style, but business letters were expected to be stilted. These are quite modest accomplishments by the standards of the later-Victorian public school or, for that matter by the standards of the Lincoln School of Science & Art at the end of the century. The problem that Hall faced was that a school of this size must inevitably do most of its teaching in a single class. This presented a massive challenge to new pupils; after a year at school they could relax; and after two years there was little more for them to learn. But in a provincial town at the start of Victoria's reign, parental expectations were low. Hall's pupils left with enough knowledge for the next stage of their journey through life; and perhaps the process of socialisation which a boarding school offered was valued as much as the academic accomplishments.

Establishing the exact location of the school is helped by what is now Manor Lane, one of the streets running westwards from High Street towards the Cliff, being recorded as Hall's Lane in the 1841 census. By this date, Robert Hall was dead. His son, John, appears in the 1841 census, described as a farmer. His entry comes, not under Hall's Lane, but under Timms Lane, the next lane to the south. The probable explanation for this is that Hall's house was that now known as Toynbee Court, which stands adjacent to Manor Lane but whose front door is reached by a driveway from Timms Lane. Not only is this house of ample size to have housed a school as well as a working farm, but there is a clear distinction between the formal garden at the front and a more utilitarian yard at the back. This would accord with the account of the squirrel that came 'out of the fir-tree into the Yard'. It also accords with an advertisement of 1840 seeking a new tenant: 'The house is capable of accommodating upwards of 50 Boarders, having good school and dining rooms, excellent airy sleeping-rooms, with a pleasant Play Ground and good Gardens, well planted with choice fruit trees.'

George Boole's school and the move to Pottergate

Bob Wheeler

Robert Hall, owner of the academy at which George Boole taught in Waddington, died on 8 August 1837, having named his son John as executor. John approached George Boole about his taking on the school, proposing that Boole should lease the premises for a term of 29 years at £110 per year. For his part, he promised there would be 30 boarders when Boole took over. The sum asked was preposterous: the house was worth something like £30, so Boole was in effect to purchase the goodwill by paying an additional £80 for 29 years. Remarkably, the great mathematician accepted these unreasonable terms, possibly from a sense of obligation to the Halls and a reluctance to haggle, so he signed the lease.

An advertisement was duly placed in the *Stamford Mercury* on 1 September, stating that the school would pass into the hands of Mr George Boole from the end of the year. The advertisement added that:

> his system of instruction, the result of some experience and much reflection, has been fully tested in the establishing and conducting of a large and respectable School in Lincoln. In proof of its superiority, whether as regards the communication of a sound English education, the higher orders of classical and mathematical literature, or, lastly, its moral character and influence, abundant testimonials can be produced.

3 Pottergate. (*Courtesy of the Heslam Trust and Electric Egg*).

It was of course the higher mathematics and, to a lesser extent, Latin and Greek that Boole was really interested in teaching, but out at Waddington he was cut off from potential day boys who might want tuition in those subjects. Numbers of boarders had perhaps declined during the autumn of 1839 when the school was being run by the assistants; certainly there were fewer than the 30 boarders promised. At the rent Boole had agreed, the school lost money. It really was a venture upon which he should never have embarked. Eventually, and after some negotiation, John Hall allowed Boole to withdraw from the lease in return for a 'substantial' payment – though the exact amount is unknown.

We have one reminiscence from this period from a pupil's viewpoint. Friday afternoon was the high point of the week. The pupils wrote letters home; then there was a lecture by Boole on some subject of popular interest like astronomy or chemistry; then came the arrival of the carrier's cart from Lincoln, with letters from home and, hopefully, something good like cake. It would seem also that Boole continued Hall's practice of birthday celebrations, now transferred to 2 November, Boole's own birthday. These involved a day's holiday, with games and a special tea (but no mention of ale).

From Easter 1840, Boole, free of his ties to John Hall, moved the school to Lincoln, to 3 Pottergate. This is a house in the Close, leased by the Dean and Chapter to Robert Hill, who had previously given dancing lessons there to the cream of youthful society but had later moved to Leamington. Boole took the house as Hill's under-tenant. The house was an L-shaped building, mostly of the early eighteenth century. The entrance was at the internal angle of the 'L' and led to a spacious entrance hall. Off to one side was a good-sized dining room and a parlour; in the short arm of the 'L' was the kitchen. There were five rooms on the first floor, with attics above. Included in the lease was a garden between the Close wall and Wragby Road, a space largely taken by road improvements in the twentieth century when the road was widened to pass to the north of Pottergate arch. This garden was linked to the house by a private passage at the back of 2 Pottergate. It must have provided a space where the boys could shout and play without disturbing the peace of the Close.

The following year's census gives a good picture of the new Lincoln establishment. George Boole lived with his parents, his sister Mary Ann, and his brother William, who was described as 'Assistant'. There were three female servants, all fairly young, and the ten pupils, all boys, were aged from ten to fifteen. The servants and the pupils are treated as separate households from the family, suggesting that there was a school dining room, separate from the family's (although it appears that Boole himself took breakfast with the boys). There is no sign of a housekeeper, so the domestic side was presumably run by his mother, assisted by her daughter. One of the oldest pupils was Elmer Brown, who may possibly be the 'Master Brown' mentioned by William Wright at Waddington in 1837; but four years was a fairly long time for a pupil to remain at the same school, and Brown is a common surname.

we assume that the servants ate their meals in the kitchen and the family ate in the parlour, the boys – the boarders, that is – could have used the dining room for their meals. The dining room, being the largest room in the house, perhaps also served as the main school room. There must have been at least one further classroom where Boole himself could teach the higher subjects; that must have been one of the first-floor rooms. Boole's parents, Boole himself, his brother and his sister would all have needed bedrooms. The boys and the female servants would no doubt have slept in the attics; the house had two staircases so it may have been possible to arrange the attics so that the boys and the young female servants had no possibility of social intercourse. These things mattered greatly. The main point to note is that the house was actually rather cramped to be a boarding school. It might have been possible to expand the number of day-boys but there was limited scope for increasing the number of boarders.

One of the ways Boole's 1840 prospectus differed from his 1839 one is that day-boys were specifically mentioned. They paid £6.6s per year. There was a small extra charge for book-keeping and for land-surveying – Boole seems not to have shared Hall's enthusiasm for these subjects. Parents probably felt differently: Boole recorded in later life that what he had been running was 'virtually a commercial school'. Of course, by the time Boole wrote this, Thomas Arnold's work at Rugby had transformed middle-class expectations of schooling: classics were now all-important, while book-keeping was disdained as a subject fit only for shop-keepers.

Boole was worried initially about attracting adequate numbers. However, there were only two other masters in the city who kept private boarding schools. Thomas Bainbridge's establishment in Michaelgate was where Boole himself had studied and it seems to have catered for the economy end of the market. The direct competitor was Rev George Rigg, a Cambridge graduate, whose school was in Newport, in the building that now houses the Lincolnshire Open Research and Innovation Centre. Boole already had a reputation as a local genius – but that did not of itself make him a good teacher. Rigg had the advantage of an established position. Location in the Close must have been one of Boole's 'selling points', to use a term he certainly would have avoided, offering convenience for day-boys and somewhere that would impress parents from outside the city looking for a boarding school. Although Boole was fairly discreet about making his charges public, it may be significant that he was undercutting Rigg, who charged basic fees of 30 guineas per year. Even as late as 1849, Boole was charging 24 to 28 guineas, depending on age. By 1841, Boole had ten boarders; Rigg had just two. In any case, in 1841 Rigg became incumbent of St Peter, Eastgate, and may have considered that the duties of an urban parish precluded his continuing to run a school. By the end of his time at Lincoln, the school was doing so well that Boole was employing no fewer than three assistants.

Another prospectus is known from 1849. The biggest change was a new category offered: parlour boarders were taken at a 50% supplement in fees. One author has described this category a 'mysterious' but Charles Dickens provides the explanation: it describes the arrangements made for David Copperfield at Dr Strong's school in Canterbury, where Copperfield was taken into the family of his aunt's lawyer. So Boole was offering to take pupils who would live as part of his family rather than living communally with their fellow-pupils. To the modern way of thinking it seems an odd arrangement, but Boole took what he termed 'private pupils', including for example a young man wanting to improve his mathematics prior to going up to Cambridge – and continuing with this arrangement during a Long Vacation; it may be that the arrangement was intended for such as these.

As for the style of Boole's teaching, in his advertisements he emphasised the importance of understanding rather than rote-learning; but the acquisition of facts clearly remained important. Boole seems to have been keen on subjecting his pupils to public examination – that is oral examination by an outside authority in the presence of an audience. Thus we read in December 1840 that 'the young gentlemen generally distinguished themselves by the prompt and distinct answers that were given, in reply to questions in arithmetic, and geometry, geography, history, and other branches of a liberal education'. It is difficult to see how this was other than a test of memory.

Boole's occasional advertisements for assistants throw light on the nature of the teaching. In 1840, an assistant was wanted for the *Writing department*. In 1844, an assistant in the English department had to be a *superior Penman*. One gains the impression that a great deal of emphasis was placed on instructing pupils in a neat copper-plate hand. It is more encouraging to read in 1844 that one of the pupils had broken his arm while playing leap-frog on the Common. One is sorry for the boy in question but it is good to know that the boys were able to let off steam somewhere more spacious than the little garden outside the Close wall.

George Boole moved to Cork in October 1849. What happened to his school? For the final quarter of 1849 it must have continued under the management of the assistants. Boole had by now assembled a capable team, including, it would seem, the younger brother of the Thomas Dyson, with whom Boole had worked in his first teaching post at Doncaster. Because Boole was in Ireland, he wisely left the commercial negotiations to Gilbert Collins, a friend who was running the Lincoln office of the Hull bank. Collins arranged a sale to one John Jackson Swift, who had spent fourteen years as an assistant master and who, it would seem, had suddenly come into money, a change in fortune which may possibly be related to his marrying the daughter of a Brigg corn-merchant. It is worth saying something about the new era, because of what the contrast tells us about Boole.

irst, Boole was intimately involved in the running of his school; in contrast, Swift went off to Trinity College Dublin for three years to take a BA, followed by a year at Durham pursuing a Licentiate in Theology – by then a prerequisite for ordination. Presumably the pupils only saw him during university vacations.

Secondly, the pupils may have been grateful for his absences, because there was a flavour of Charles Dickens' Mr Creakle about him: he introduced 'the flogging system', something about which Boole was pained to learn.

Thirdly, Swift was a master of 'spin'. Whereas Boole in his advertisements struggled bravely to set out his philosophy of education in a manner which probably confused most parents, Swift would string together all the best phrases into a description that was elegantly composed but said nothing.

THE REV. J. J. SWIFT, A.M., prepares pupils for the active pursuits of life, by inculcating Moral and Religious Principles, as the ground-work of a thorough and sound Education, imparted on a liberal and comprehensive system, which long and varied experience has enabled the Advertiser to adopt with unfailing success.

This example is from later years, when he was vicar of Cherry Willingham. It sounds splendid, but what does it mean?

George Boole and the Lincoln Mechanics' Institute

Lesley Clarke

The mechanics' institutes, or institutions (both terms are used here depending on the source consulted) were one of the nineteenth-century organisations aiming to educate working men, and became particularly necessary as an increasingly industrialised workforce called for workers who could maintain and repair their machinery. This, together with the ideal of social improvement during the 1830s and 1840s, led to the rapid expansion of mechanics' institutes and by the second half of the nineteenth century there were about 1200 in Great Britain. The first known use of the term was the Glasgow Mechanics' Institution, formed around 1823.

On 26 October 1833, a requisition was made to the Mayor of Lincoln to convene a public meeting to consider the establishment of a mechanics' institute in Lincoln. The requisition was signed by 184 people including John and William Boole (most likely George's father John, and his uncle William, who for many years had been a teacher at a school in Bassingham). The mayor consented and the meeting was held in the 'Guild-Hall' on 31 October 1833, when it was unanimously agreed that a mechanics' institution should be established in Lincoln and that:

> the objects of the Lincoln and Lincolnshire Mechanics' Institution shall be the Cultivation of Experimental, Natural, and Moral Philosophy; and of Useful Knowledge, in all departments, avoiding Politics and controversial Divinity.

As to premises, fortuitously the ground floor of Greyfriars on Free School Lane had been vacated in 1831 by the Jersey School, their knitting and spinning work being taken over by machines. At meetings on 11 and 20 December 1833, it was agreed these premises were the best that could be found; described as 'that ancient, respectable, and interesting building'. A rent of £10 *per annum* was fixed, but would be met by the Corporation. A total of £100 was needed to form three classrooms, a library and accommodation for the librarian or curator. Permission was also granted for use of the grammar school above as a lecture room, which would accommodate up to 250 people. George's father, John Boole, was appointed curator in April 1834, but resigned in December 1835.

By 1834 George Boole had returned to Lincoln from his teaching positions in Doncaster, Liverpool and Waddington and was deeply involved in the newly-formed Institute. He was a supporter of the ideal of social improvement and keen to help those less fortunate than himself, particularly through education. George Boole served as an unpaid teacher for many years, and became a committed member of the Institute.

George Boole's first-known lecture to the Mechanics' Institute took place in their lecture room on 5 February 1835 and was entitled *On the Genius and Discoveries of Sir Isaac Newton*. This was held

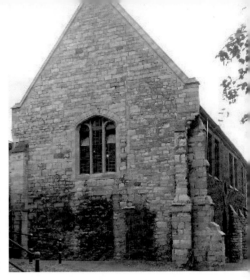

Greyfriars, home of the Mechanics' Institute.
Lesley Clarke).

to celebrate the unveiling of a marble bust of Newton recently acquired for the reading room. Although only 19 years of age and relatively recently involved with the Institute, Boole was chosen to give this lecture in recognition of the impact he had already made on that institution. His lecture was well received, published later in 1835 and sold in Lincoln and London.

Boole was very interested in the Institute's library and in 1846 submitted a report noting in particular the lack of books on the mathematical sciences. Whilst appreciating that such books would require a degree of time and attention on the part of the readers, he nevertheless thought it would be worthwhile to add them to the library in case 'exceptional individuals' wished to use them. Boole disagreed with the rule forbidding works on party politics and controversial theology from being included in the library, considering it an infringement of personal liberty. In 1846, by which time there was more religious tolerance in general, Boole delivered a lecture to the Lincoln Mechanics' Institute entitled *A Plea for Freedom* expressing his disagreement with the rule, particularly regarding religion, believing that discussion of religion was the way to truth. Boole's own religious beliefs are not clear. Although he showed a leaning towards Unitarianism, this did not grow into a strong affiliation.

Acknowledging the necessity of leisure time in order to study, George Boole became involved in the Lincoln Early Closing Association which in early 1847 achieved the introduction of the ten-hour working day for all shop assistants, apprentices and other workers in the city of Lincoln. Boole was asked to give a lecture in celebration, which he did on Friday, 9 February 1847. Entitled *The Right Use of Leisure*, the lecture was given in the City Assembly Rooms above the Buttermarket in Silver Street.

As George Boole prepared to leave Lincoln in 1849, to take up his professorship of mathematics at Queen's College, Cork, he became aware that the members of the Lincoln Mechanics' Institute were proposing a parting gift. According to a meeting held on the 15th anniversary of the Lincoln & Lincolnshire Mechanics' Institution, 1848, the gift was to be 'a handsome testimonial ... in the form of a costly and elegantly-bound volume, being a copy of *Johnston's Physical Atlas*.' In a letter dated 22 August 1849 addressed to the Lincoln Mechanics' Institute, Boole expressed his gratitude but said he would rather the money was put towards the purchase of an astronomical telescope larger than the one they owned, or the purchase of the entire works of Newton for the library, offering to make up the amount needed for Newton's works. He added that, if they still insisted he should have a token of their good wishes, he would suggest a small inkstand, without inscription, at a value not exceeding a few shillings. His feelings on this subject were rather beautifully described thus: 'You will agree with me that upon an occasion such as this the sentiment and the regard from which the act emanates are everything – the act itself nothing.'

However, despite his protestations, George Boole was presented with many gifts, including Johnston's *Atlas* from the Institute, during a public supper held in his honour at *The White Hart* on Friday 28 December 1849.

The Mechanics' Institution continued in Greyfriars until 1858, when its rooms were required for the expanding school. It moved to the Buttermarket on Silver Street, but was ousted from there in 1891 when those premises were required for the New Free Library. The Mechanics' Institute continued in other premises until 1899, but by then its usefulness was outlived. The 12,000 books in its library were sold and the Lincoln Mechanics' Institution was closed. However, its plaque still remains on the south wall of Greyfriars, inscribed:-

> Mechanics Institution
> MDCCCXXXIII

Mechanics' Institution plaque.
(*Lesley Clarke*).

Accommodating a thirst for knowledge in George Boole's Lincoln

Andrew Walker

George Boole played an active part in many of the growing number of knowledge-based clubs, associations and societies that developed in Lincoln, alongside many other urban centres, during the first half of the nineteenth century. Amongst the societies with which George Boole was involved was the Lincolnshire Topographical Society, which was set up at a meeting attended by a 'Mr Boole' on 18 January 1841. The aim of the society, according to the *Stamford Mercury* on 22 January 1841, was for its members, paying a fairly substantial subscription of 10 shillings a year, 'to acquire and record information connected with history, antiquities, geology, statistics and topography of the county of Lincoln'.

Accommodating the needs of such clubs, associations and societies were a number of variously-sized rooms across the city, which could be rented out as needed. In the case of the Lincolnshire Topographical Society, its first meetings took place in 'Mr Spray's Rooms', variously described in newspaper reports as 'above hill' or on Bailgate. By the time of the Society's second annual general meeting, larger accommodation was required. This meeting was held at the City Assembly Rooms, located in a notoriously-chilly space immediately above the Butter Market, situated on the High Street, next to St Peter-at-Arches' Church, near the High Street's junction with Silver Street. The Butter Market was built in 1757 and had a fine Portland stone pediment, with a tympanum in which the arms of the city were displayed. Whilst the building no longer exists, having been demolished to allow the High Street to be widened, its façade was relocated and became the front of a new Central Market, opened in 1938 in what is now City Square.

The City Assembly Rooms were funded by public subscription and, in 1838, the *Lincolnshire Chronicle*, reported that the venue and associated card room were 'kept in good repair'. According to Thomas Allen's *History of the County of Lincoln, Volume I*, published in 1834, the interior of the venue was 'fitted up with much taste and the principal room contains three recesses with large bronze statues given by Lady Monson in 1813.' By 1843, however, Lincoln Town Council met to discuss the need for repairs to the building, which was partly used as a people's news room. The committee set up to oversee repairs indicated that if the rooms were to continue to be used for cheap suppers, smoking and other 'populous meetings', then funds would not be donated to refurbishing the structure. In the event, repairs did take place and White's 1856 *Directory of Lincolnshire* declared that the City Assembly Rooms had been 'lately tastefully re-decorated'. George Boole was a regular visitor to the City Assembly Rooms in order to attend meetings. It was a facility with which he was familiar as it was only a few minutes' walk from his childhood home at 49 Silver Street, as Beryl George indicates in her chapter on 'Lincoln's changing centre'. One of his last appearances there as a resident of Lincoln was to give a lecture on the 'right use and improvement of leisure generally' in February 1847.

The City Assembly Rooms were the second assembly rooms to be built in Lincoln. The first such rooms to be constructed were the County Assembly Rooms, located on the east side of Bailgate and built by Abraham Hayward in 1744. Hayward was a local builder, who had built Disney Place on Eastgate eight years earlier. During the eighteenth century, many mid-ranking towns, especially county towns, enjoyed what one historian, Peter Borsay, has referred to as an 'urban renaissance'. In order to meet the needs of the landed classes and urban ruling classes for recreation and culture many towns extended their public leisure provision, with the development, or extension, of racecourses, theatres and meeting places, such as assembly rooms. Lincoln's was amongst the first major assembly rooms constructed, succeeding the building at York, built in 1732, but preceding the Bath Assembly Rooms, opened in 1771. Lincoln's County Assembly Rooms was financed through subscriptions, gathered principally from the county's landed families.

The assembly rooms of a town or city often accommodated prestigious social events attracting visitors well beyond the urban centre itself. The annual event with which Lincoln's County Assembly Rooms became particularly associated was the Lincolnshire Stuff Ball. This was a social occasion, attracting members of most of the county's landed families and had been initiated to encourage the use of Lincolnshire-made woollens, at a time when the county's textile industry was struggling. No lady was to be admitted to the ball who did not wear a dress verified as being made of Lincolnshire wool (known as 'stuff').

The County Assembly Rooms, Bailgate. (*Adam O'Meara*).

Whilst the Stuff Ball was not likely to feature prominently within George Boole's social calendar, the County Assembly Rooms also accommodated a range of activities which might have attracted his attention. During the 1830s and 1840s for instance, the venue regularly housed meetings and other activities associated with Lincoln Choral Society and the Lincolnshire Architectural Society. In 1848, the County Assembly Rooms was the principal base for the visit by the Archaeological Institute of Great Britain and Ireland, which is described in Michael J. Jones's chapter.

Other Lincoln-based organisations and locations closely associated with the accumulation of knowledge with which George Boole would have been aware included a number of newsrooms. These were venues at which readers could access a wide range of newspapers and other periodicals, at a time when significant stamp duties were applied to newspapers which, deliberately on the part of government, made many of them out of reach of the pockets of working people. Stamp duties were removed by the Chancellor of the Exchequer, William Gladstone in 1855. During George Boole's time as a Lincoln inhabitant, there were several newsrooms in the city. By July 1846, according to the *Lincolnshire Chronicle*, there were four such facilities open in the city. One of the longest surviving examples in Lincoln was the City Newsroom, which was begun in 1793 and continued in operation until 1843. By 1838, a People's Newsroom was opened in the City Assembly Rooms and operated for a short time. This had initially been established by patrons of a liberal political inclination, including Sir Edward Bulwer-Lytton and Earl Yarborough. Having struggled to establish itself financially, it was removed to more modest quarters and named the *Pig and Whistle* news room. It was defunct by 1848. A County Newsroom, located in uphill Lincoln lasted longer, acquiring premises in Castle Hill in 1843 and remaining in business until 1851. Other commercial newsrooms were established such as at 28 Steep Hill, where at Mr Bellatti's a bookseller', Robert Goodacre set up a branch of the Railway Express Newsroom by October 1847, just over a year after the opening of Lincoln's first railway station by the Midland Railway Company in August 1846. Goodacre would have been known to George Boole as both served on the council of the Lincoln Topographical Society. Indeed, in November 1841 Robert Goodacre and George Boole both delivered papers at the same Topographical Society meeting – respectively on 'certain local prejudices in regard to lunar influence' and 'Druidical remains'. Goodacre's newsroom advertised three daily papers and 'an abundance of provincial and London weekly papers', with a subscription of 2s.6d. It was noted that the London morning papers were received in Lincoln by 2.00pm 'by railway express'.

Another key source of information in Lincoln during George Boole's period as a resident was the Lincoln Library. It was begun in 1814 and had 230 members by 1827 including the gentry, clergy, merchants and tradesmen, providing access by this time to some 6000 books. By 1826, according to White's Directory of the County of Lincoln, there were four subscription libraries operating in Lincoln, including the Lincoln Library. Others were located in the vestry of St Martin's Church, established in 1822; one in Butcher Lane, entitled the New Permanent Library, formed in 1822, and the Medical Library, founded in 1825.

The Lincoln Library holdings were somewhat larger than the library of Lincoln's Mechanics' Institute, with which George Boole was much associated. This had some 3000 volumes by the mid-1830s, including books previously comprising the New Permanent Library collection which had been taken over by the Mechanics' Institute. The Lincoln Library moved from its eight-yard frontage on the High Street, occupied in 1844 by the draper George Bainbridge, to new, larger premises in 1841, in a substantial building at number 278 High Street, on the corner of High Street and the northern side of Mint Lane. The library, situated immediately above a shop, was 42 feet long, 26 feet wide and 19 feet in height, with a gallery, a spacious committee room and residential quarters for the sub-librarian. It was built in an Italianate style to the plans of the architects W.A. Nicholson and Henry Goddard, both of whom were known to Boole, not least through their attendance at Topographical Society meetings. Nicholson and Goddard were treasurer and secretary respectively of the society in 1841. According to a report in the *Lincolnshire Chronicle* which described both the library's 30-feet frontage on the High Street and 80-feet long presence on Mint Lane, it was a 'matter of regret that one of the finest facades in the county should not have a more favourable position'. This Lincoln Library – sometimes called the Permanent Library – continued in operation until 1909, when much of its stock was taken over by the city's public library.

Within the city, therefore, during the first half of the nineteenth century there was a vital, developing and quickly-changing array of organisations and institutions able to feed the intellectual needs of the city's growing male population, including George Boole. Women's thirst for knowledge within the city, however, as in most early nineteenth-century urban centres, was much less well-served.

THE PROVINCIAL PRESS AND LOCAL AND REGIONAL LIFE DURING THE FIRST HALF OF THE NINETEENTH CENTURY

Andrew J.H. Jackson

Insight into the years in which George Boole was resident in Lincoln can be found through reference to the pages of the provincial press of the period. The newspapers that concerned themselves with the city and wider county provide some illuminating information on local and regional life through the first half of the nineteenth century. In Lincolnshire, as elsewhere in Britain, an older generation of generally county-town based publications had survived through from the preceding century, if not many in number. The *Stamford Mercury* was among these, claiming a lineage back into the eighteenth century. Others came to join these longer-standing newspapers in the early nineteenth century. By the time Boole left the city in 1849, there had come into being a set of further publications, for example: the *Lincoln Herald*, in print from 1828 until its move to Boston in 1832; the *Lincolnshire Chronicle*, from 1833; the *Lincoln Standard*, from 1836; and, from 1847, the *Lincolnshire Times*. George Boole was evidently aware of these newspapers. He was a young contributor to the *Lincoln Herald*, in which his verse translation from Greek of the poem, *Ode to the Spring*, was published in 1830, when he was just 14 years old. These press newcomers were attracted in a similar way to the roles and opportunities associated with conveying, promoting, celebrating, and, if appropriate, critiquing all aspects of local political, social, economic and cultural life. They also aimed to optimise and capitalise upon advertising and sales revenues; and, in addition, embark upon a political, if not necessarily a radical or stridently partisan, project. Boole would leave Lincoln at the dawn of a period of even greater expansion and optimism for the provincial press nationally, stimulated and driven forward by a combination of a more benign fiscal climate, technological advance, including significant transport developments, mounting literacy levels and reader demand, a broadening democracy, and rapid urbanisation. This later phase ushered in another round of arrivals onto the local-press scene, if half a century later, including the county's *Echo* from 1893 and Lincoln's *Leader* from 1896. Such titles adopted many of the functions and aspirations of the provincial press that had been tried and tested earlier in the century.

The columns of the provincial press describe a city and county which its residents, like Boole, knew and experienced, and to which they felt belonging or found association with, personal and collective. The newspapers discussed the character and fortunes of: political parties and units of municipal government, and their representatives; businesses, economic activities and commercial networks; social institutions and organisations; and cultural practices and beliefs. The development of local culture, its infrastructure and expression, is of particular interest and relevance in seeking to understand the Lincoln and Lincolnshire of the early decades of the nineteenth century. Moreover, the press was on hand to capture and communicate its growth and vitality. Education, training, learning, religion and philosophical debate, and other different and diverse aspects of cultural and intellectual life in general, attracted the interest of the editors of the local press, as well its readers and consumers. Indeed provincial newspapers generally were themselves a symbol the enhancement of local civic culture, as in Lincoln. The contents of the *Stamford Mercury* an *Lincolnshire Chronicle*, for example, reflect well how the local and regional newspaper media attune itself to market demand and reader interests.

In Boole's early years, from the date of his birth in 1815, provincial newspaper readers in Lincol could turn to *The Lincoln, Rutland, and Stamford Mercury*, a well-established weekly publicatio printed in Stamford. The edition opening the year 1815, of 6 January, illustrates what woul generally be found by way of content in such papers. It was a typical county-wide media output o the period – it would be some decades later before urban centres like Lincoln would acquire the scal and character to support titles with a more localised, city-specific focus. It should be noted that on of the chief cultural functions of these early regional publications was to act as a national press fo its readers, before the appearance later in the nineteenth century of the metropolitan-based dailies Editors of broadsheets like the *Mercury* assumed the task of constructing for a provincial readership a flavour of 'British' and international news from elsewhere, undertaken by extracting material from

A busy commercial scene: Lincoln High Street with stalls. Drawn by John Bartlett, 1829.
(Reproduced with permission of Lincolnshire Archives, Lincolnshire County Council. LCL7176).

ther publications. For 6 January 1815, for example, a column leads off by making reference to the headlines of the *Bristol Mirror*, while a parallel feature summarises from 'the French papers' what was significant by way of 'foreign intelligence'. More generally the publication provides a region-wide overview. Information on the cultural life of Lincoln is to be found piecemeal among numerous notices and accounts from places and districts across the county, including: births, marriages and deaths; appointments to incumbencies; 'society' events; meetings of hunts; and reports from schools. Alongside are other items relating to matters of social and economic interest, for example: court proceedings and the latest crimes; alongside bankruptcies, prices, and advertisements for medical cures. The language of the newspaper is overwhelmingly factual and informative. However, there are the occasional articles that lend themselves to a more subjective and opinion-forming style. This early January edition provides for its readership a review of the first number of a new series on *The Evidences of the Christian Religion*. The issue, in the *Mercury's* view, would 'put into the hands of every class of readers such works as will enable them to answer all cavils and objections, and effectually to instruct themselves in all the arguments upon which rests the basis of the Christian faith'.

By 1849, the year of Boole's departure from Lincoln, the *Mercury* had been joined by another Stamford-based countywide publication, *The Lincolnshire Chronicle, and Northampton, Rutland and Nottingham Advertiser*. Newspapers in general had also grown in size, and the *Chronicle* of 28 December in that year contained eight sides of newsprint, twice as many as the early January 1815 edition of the *Mercury*. The *Chronicle* of late 1849 incorporated much that would have been familiar to readers of earlier nineteenth century regional newspapers in terms of factual reporting on local cultural, political, social and economic life. However, the greater expanse of mid-century press outputs gave their readers considerably more volume of content, and, correspondingly, fuller insights into local life. Notices, accounts and viewpoints are diverse. The first column of the paper calls for subscribers to a full-length portrait of Lord Yarborough from the Directors of the Lincoln Corn Exchange; the members being 'desirous' of this end, and finding 'Noblemen, Gentlemen, and Agriculturalists' similarly disposed. The first page elsewhere is concerned with local financial and commercial reports and notices. The second page is given over to wider news: columns on 'Foreign Intelligence' turn mainly to France, and 'Domestic Intelligence' to the life of members of the royal family; followed by subsequent columns on 'Railway Intelligence' and matters 'Ecclesiastical'. The third page again is pre-occupied primarily with wider national content, political and legal, although a column is devoted to correspondence, which in this case finds the issue of free trade the main focus. Social and cultural life attracts greater attention subsequently, with reference to a musical concert in the Assembly Rooms and to the Cake Ball in the City Rooms, and the familiar feature of notices of births, marriages and deaths.

By the end of the nineteenth century, town- and city-focussed newspapers giving over great content to local news were more widespread. Nonetheless, in the first half of the century, Linco. residents like Boole witnessed the emergence of a provincial press aiming to keep its readersh abreast of wider political and economic issues, debates and trends, and aware of local social an cultural events, opportunities, experiences and ideas.

George Boole and the Chartist

Richard Skipworth

The paths of George Boole and the Chartist, Thomas Cooper, intersected for a period and each left pen pictures of the other. Thomas Cooper first came across 14 year-old George Boole in the Christmas week of 1829. Thomas Cooper, then aged 24, was visiting Lincoln, courting his future wife, Susanna Chaloner, George Boole's cousin. In his autobiography, Cooper wrote:

> Young George came to see his cousins ... (he) had mastered *Leslie's Geometry*, under his father's teaching, was learning Latin and thinking of Greek; and almost overwhelmed me with enquiries about the contents of books he had not read.

Cooper, of course, was not at this time a Chartist. The *People's Charter*, with its six points (demanding votes for all men, secret ballots, no property qualifications, payment of MPs, constituencies of equal size, and annual parliaments), was not published until 1838. Nevertheless, he did hold some radical political views. Born in Leicester in 1805, Cooper spent most of his childhood in Gainsborough, brought up by his mother, a dyer by occupation. His mother, whilst very supportive of Thomas's education, could not teach him directly unlike John Boole, George Boole's father. Both Thomas Cooper and George Boole, however, quickly developed a ferocious and voracious interest in all aspects of learning.

Greyfriars from the south, prior to the construction of the present St Swithin's Church in 1870. (*Maurice Hodson collection*).

In Cooper's case this included politics. In Gainsborough 'there was a shop of brushmakers very close to us and they were the most determined politicians.' They introduced him to the writings of William Cobbett and Henry 'Orator' Hunt. He came to hate the prime minister Lord Liverpool and his government and to believe that all the sufferings of the poor were attributable to them. (Lord Liverpool introduced a range of repressive measures, particularly following the Peterloo massacre in 1819, when, at a large radical meeting in Manchester, 18 people were killed and up to 700 were injured following a cavalry charge.)

George Boole was also interested in the social problems of the age but he supported causes that aimed to help the individual rather than the wholesale social change advocated by Thomas Cooper. He was involved in setting up the Female Penitents' Home on Carline Road in Lincoln which aimed to restore 'females who have deviated from the paths of virtue ... to a reputable position in society'. He was a Vice-President of the Early Closing Association in Lincoln which campaigned to reduce hours of work to improve the health of workers. When in 1847 a ten-hour day was introduced for workers in Lincoln, he gave a celebrated lecture at the Lincoln Mechanics' Institute (*The Right Use of Leisure*): 'I address myself this evening to the young men of Lincoln, and more especially to that portion of them who have benefited by the late movement for the early closing of shops'.

Both George Boole and Thomas Cooper were supporters of the Lincoln Mechanics' Institute, examined in Lesley Clarke's chapter, a forerunner of adult education set up in 1833. When Thomas Cooper moved to Lincoln in 1834 he joined the Mechanics' Institute and was soon on the committee along with both John Boole ('Curator') and George Boole (committee member and later 'Superintendent of Instruction'). Cooper came to admire George Boole's formidable intellect. He was particularly impressed by another lecture (*An Address on the Genius and Discoveries of Sir Isaac Newton*) given by Boole to the Mechanics' Institute on 5 February 1835. Though he noted that Boole was 'shy and formal ... [he] was as good as he was great'. Boole, on the other hand, writing in 1847 to his friend E.R. Larken, admired Cooper for being 'honest and sincere and open'. He might be 'vain and perhaps pedantic' but he had a lot to be vain about.

In 1838 Cooper left Lincoln, moving first to London and then on to Leicester. Here he became fully involved with the Chartists, eventually touring the country as a powerful advocate of the movement. This led to his downfall since, after he addressed a meeting in the Potteries, there was a full-scale riot. Cooper was wrongly blamed and sentenced to two years in prison for conspiracy and sedition.

Cooper's activities and time in prison did not seem to have led to his being ostracised by the Boole family or other intellectual acquaintances in Lincoln. Whilst in prison Cooper had composed a lengthy poem, *The Purgatory of Suicides: A Prison-Rhyme*, which set out the case for Chartism.

When asked to comment on the poem prior to a second edition being prepared, George Boole was happy to do so. He admired the poem's beauty and seriousness of intent though noted 'bitternesses' and felt that in general the poem was an 'unhealthy' one. Writing to his friend E.R. Larken, Rector of Burton (the village near Lincoln), Boole sought his comments to pass on to Cooper as Larken had 'read the poem with much more care than I.'

It is perhaps surprising that such 'rebel' literature as this poem was well known to both of these apparently conventional Victorian men. Boole, however, had earlier revealed himself to be a strong supporter of freedom of thought and expression in a talk to the Mechanics' Institute (*A Plea for Freedom*). The constitution of the Mechanics' Institute banned from its library works that were political or that involved controversial theology. Boole argued that it would be difficult to find works that had no political or religious import and that members of the Institute should be involved in the great debates of the age: 'On its silent shelves the Free Trader and the Protectionist, the feudalist and the advocate of change, should array their facts and marshal their arguments, for the effectual battle of Truth.'

Cooper outlived Boole by many years, living on into the final decade of the nineteenth century. In his early years, Christianity had been very important to Cooper. He had joined the Primitive Methodists and then switched to the Wesleyan Methodists, becoming a preacher. After he moved to Lincoln, he became sceptical about Christianity, influenced by the writings of David Strauss. In the late 1850s he rejected his scepticism and in 1859 became a Baptist. Once again he toured the country this time speaking up for Christianity rather than Chartism. When the Baptists decided in 1884 to build a new chapel in Lincoln it was named in his honour. The chapel was originally in St Benedict's Square in Lincoln but, in 1972, following the building's demolition, a new Baptist church was built on Lincoln's High Street and still bears his name. Cooper died in 1892. His memorial is in Canwick Road Cemetery, Lincoln. The headstone also commemorates his wife Susanna Cooper and her sister, Letitia Swann, a straw bonnet maker.

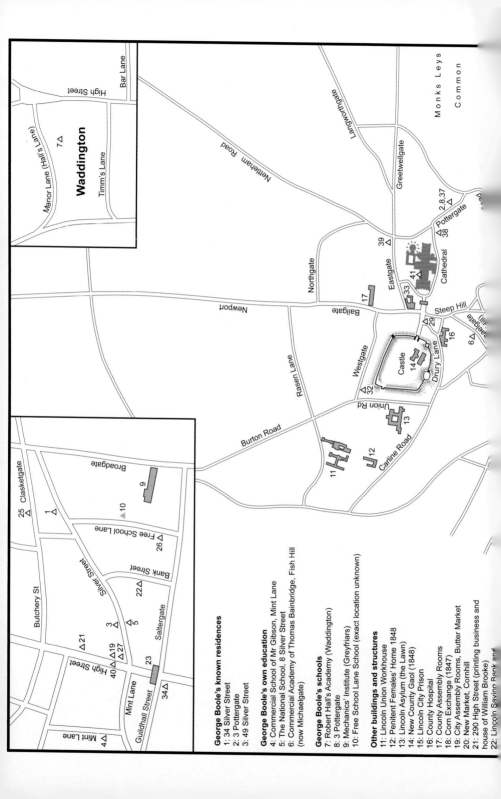

Waddington

Manor Lane (Hall's Lane)
High Street
Bar Lane
Timm's Lane
7 △

Monks Leys Common

Langworthgate
Greetwellgate
Nettleham Road
2,8,37
Pottergate
38
39
Eastgate
Cathedral
Northgate
33
41
Newport
Bailgate
17
Steep Hill
Westgate
29
16
Rasen Lane
Castle
14
Drury Lane
9
Burton Road
32
Union Rd
13
Carline Road
12
11

Clasketgate
25 △
Broadgate
1 △
9
Free School Lane
10 ▲
26 ▽
Butchery St
Silver Street
Bank Street
22 △
Saltergate
3 △
5 △
21 △
40 △
19 △
27 △
High Street
23
Mint Lane
34 △
4 ▽
Guildhall Street

George Boole's known residences
1: 34 Silver Street
2: 3 Pottergate
3: 49 Silver Street

George Boole's own education
4: Commercial School of Mr Gibson, Mint Lane
5: The National School, 8 Silver Street
6: Commercial Academy of Thomas Bainbridge, Fish Hill (now Michaelgate)

George Boole's schools
7: Robert Hall's Academy (Waddington)
8: 3 Pottergate
9: Mechanics' Institute (Greyfriars)
10: Free School Lane School (exact location unknown)

Other buildings and structures
11: Lincoln Union Workhouse
12: Penitent Females' Home 1848
13: Lincoln Asylum (the Lawn)
14: New County Gaol (1848)
15: Lincoln City Prison
16: County Hospital
17: County Assembly Rooms
18: Corn Exchange (1847)
19: City Assembly Rooms, Butter Market
20: New Market, Cornhill
21: 290 High Street (printing business and house of William Brooke)
22: Lincoln Saving Bank and

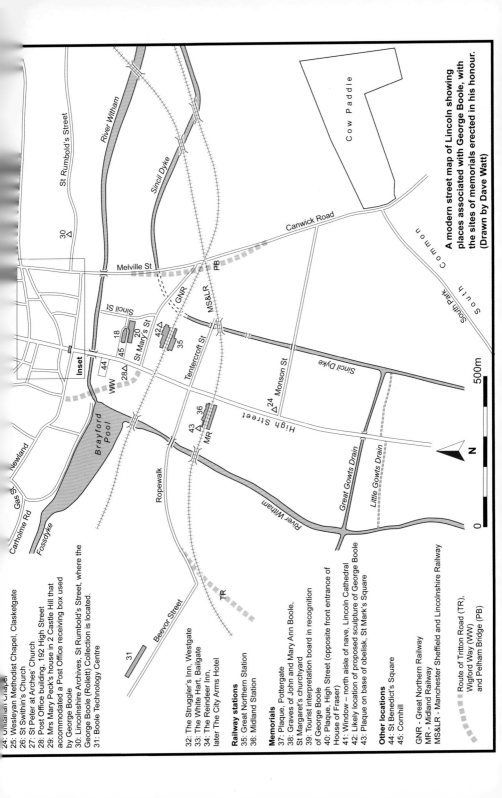

24: Unitarian Chapel
25: Wesleyan Methodist Chapel, Claskergate
26: St Swithin's Church
27: St Peter at Arches' Church
28: Post Office building, 192 High Street
29: Mrs Mary Peck's house in 2 Castle Hill that
accommodated a Post Office receiving box used
by George Boole
30: Lincolnshire Archives, St Rumbold's Street, where the
George Boole (Rollett) Collection is located.
31: Boole Technology Centre

32: The Struggler's Inn, Westgate
33: The White Hart, Bailgate
34: The Reindeer Inn,
later The City Arms Hotel

Railway stations
35: Great Northern Station
36: Midland Station

Memorials
37: Plaque, Pottergate
38: Graves of John and Mary Ann Boole,
St Margaret's churchyard
39: Tourist interpretation board in recognition
of George Boole
40: Plaque, High Street (opposite front entrance of
House of Fraser)
41: Window – north aisle of nave, Lincoln Cathedral
42: Likely location of proposed sculpture of George Boole
43: Plaque on base of obelisk, St Mark's Square

Other locations
44: St Benedict's Square
45: Cornhill

GNR - Great Northern Railway
MR - Midland Railway
MS&LR - Manchester Sheffield and Lincolnshire Railway

▪▪▪▪ Route of Tritton Road (TR),
Wigford Way (WW)
and Pelham Bridge (PB)

A modern street map of Lincoln showing
places associated with George Boole, with
the sites of memorials erected in his honour.
(Drawn by Dave Watt)

The Lincoln Saving Bank and Lincoln Benefit Building Society

Geoff Tann

The Lincoln Saving Bank was, according to the *Stamford Mercury* on 2 February 1816, the product of 'some benevolent gentlemen of Lincoln and the neighbourhood promoting the establishment of a bank for the receipt and augmentation of the humble savings of the poor'. Under the patronage of Lady Monson, with Charles Chaplin MP as President and Charles Sibthorp MP as Treasurer, the bank was established at a meeting in Lincoln's Guildhall on 26 March 1816 and opened at the National School for transactions on Saturday 6 April 1816, 6pm – 8pm. In July they extended their offering by opening on Fridays 1-2pm and Saturdays 7-8pm for members who lived in the country.

A clerk was appointed in 1826, with an auditor appointed shortly afterwards. The first paid auditor was George Boole's father, John, who held the role of clerk and auditor in 1828 after depositing a security of £100. In addition to his pay, he was granted an additional £10 *per annum* for recording descriptions of the depositors who were unable to write. John Boole continued as auditor until early 1847 when he resigned 'after about twenty years' because of his severe ill health, and died in December 1848. His role was divided between two post holders – an auditor and a clerk – elected in March 1847.

George Boole appears to have had no involvement with the bank, but this was possibly connected with the need for financial probity and the avoidance of any conflict of interest with the auditor. The bank moved from the National School premises in 1838 to Bank Street, where they converted a house and former vestry room of a Wesleyan chapel. These buildings were partly damaged by a bomb in January 1943 but were restored in 1952. More extensive alterations and demolitions were conducted as part of the 1957 construction of the (now redundant) Trustees Savings Bank building designed by Hull architects Wheatley and Houldsworth.

The first Lincoln Benefit Building Society developed from a well-attended public meeting on 7 December 1846 at the City Assembly Rooms, when Rev. E. R. Larken of Burton village spoke about forming a mutual improvement society for 'providing houses for the working classes'. The working model envisaged the Society lasting for twelve years. Resolutions to create the Lincoln Building Society were passed and a list of potential members was made at the end of the meeting. Eighty shareholders were signed up in the first week and about 90 members attended a meeting which was held at the Saltergate Billiard Rooms on 21 December. Although the initial name persisted in use, the organisation became known as the Lincoln Benefit Building Society in time for the first shareholders' meeting, held on 18 January 1847, at number 2 Saltergate. Directors were appointed at that meeting and then held their first Directors' meeting on 23 January 1847. Loans for land and buildings were provided in March.

George Boole's documented association with the building society occurred as a result of a resolution passed at the annual meeting in January 1848 when it was agreed to promote the society with a public meeting. A subsequent meeting in the vestry room of Mint Lane Chapel on 17 March questioned the need for extra promotion, arguing against it on the grounds of expense and the risk that the meeting would be perceived negatively as an appeal for funds. It is recorded that Rev. John Cross (of Mint Lane Chapel) and George Boole addressed the meeting, but their arguments are not known. The meeting unanimously agreed that the public meeting would not proceed.

The building society was disbanded earlier than expected in January 1857 after only ten years, but another similar society replaced it and continued its successes.

The arrival of the railways

Adam Cartwright

By the 1830s and early 1840s, longer distance travel from Lincoln had significantly improved: no to levels that we would find acceptable today, of course, but the city was well served with road transport links, by which it was possible to reach a wide variety of locations more quickly than eve before. The more adventurous traveller could even take a boat to London, changing to a steamer at Hobhole Sluice on the Witham Haven below Boston, or going north to pick up a steamship at Hull, but that was a less predictable and usually longer trip. For a progressive young man such as George Boole, who wanted to mix with fellow men of learning – and meantime find employment in his early profession as a schoolmaster – these choices of service were very welcome.

Boole was only 16 years old when he was engaged as an usher at Heigham's School, Doncaster. Some 40 miles distant, the Yorkshire town situated on the Great North Road was a major stage carriage hub, and George would have had no difficulty in finding a coach service north from Lincoln. He may just have preferred a cheaper alternative by taking a series of local carriers north, or even a sloop down the Fossdyke to Torksey, on to Gainsborough or Goole and thence to Doncaster.

George Boole was invited to Cambridge in 1839 by Duncan Gregory, the mathematician and first editor of the *Cambridge Mathematical Journal*. Fortunately, a direct coach had recently been started from Lincoln to the university city, leaving the *Spread Eagle Hotel* in Lincoln High Street at 5.30am, taking the Great North Road down to Stamford and on to Huntingdon finally arriving in Cambridge at 6pm that evening, having taken just over 12 hours to cover the (almost) 100 miles.

The gradual expansion of the national railway network in the 1830s reduced the need for such extended coach journeys since it became easier to run coach services to the nearest railway station. With the partial opening of the London & Birmingham Railway in April 1838, a new coach was introduced to convey Lincoln passengers to a temporary station at Denbigh Hall, a short-lived affair a mile north of Bletchley in Buckinghamshire, and then to Euston. Leaving Lincoln at 6am, the

total journey took 15 hours, depositing exhausted passengers in the capital at 9pm. Despite this arduous proposition, the route was popular although offering little advantage – no more than an hour or so – over the more direct coach route. The opening of a new railway from Northampton to Peterborough in 1845 prompted a diversion of some coach routes to Wansford station on the Great North Road, near Stamford, with Peterborough station another alternative. This reduced travelling time only a little to between 10

Midland Railway Station (later St Mark's): the classical façade. (*Rob Wheeler*).

Great Northern Station (now Lincoln Central). (*Dave Prichard*).

and 11 hours, with a further reduction by November 1845 to just under 10 hours if travelling via Nottingham railway station by the *Prince Albert* coach from the *Saracen's Head Hotel*.

When the Lincoln and Nottingham (later Midland) Railway opened its station at St Mark's in August 1846, the fastest service to London cut two hours off the journey. Leaving Lincoln at a more bearable 8am, passengers could reach Euston by 3.45pm. Whilst this was better than the previous road – rail offerings, necessary changes of train at Trent Junction and Rugby prevented a meaningful difference in time. It was only with the opening of the more direct Great Northern Railway via Boston and Peterborough in 1848, and the introduction of through trains to London in 1850, that appreciable improvements became possible. By 1851 the GNR was delivering its Lincoln customers to London in just under four hours. In the space of 14 years, the journey time had been cut by two thirds.

These advances were not without their drawbacks. Building both railways in a busy city within a few years of each other was very disruptive, especially to the lower High Street, where the Midland and then Great Northern (then London and York Railway) stations were to be constructed. The land acquired for the Midland station alone, including Mr Douthwaite's orchard stretching between High Street and the River Witham, comprised more than ten acres and cost over £18,000. Lincoln's first railway station had temporary buildings; construction of the stone and brick main buildings continued during the year. No sooner was the Midland station complete than construction started in spring 1847 on the Great Northern railway through the city. Initial clearance activity involved the demolition of buildings standing in the way of progress, marked by the virtual collapse, in March 1847, of a dilapidated house formerly occupied by the surgeon James Marr Snow. A wide range of structures had to be removed to make way for the Great Northern station, including a brewhouse, various warehouses, a granary, stables and several yards. From the establishment of a ballast pit at Boultham to the purchase of 28 acres of the Holmes pastures, to creating a railway yard (now the Brayford Pool campus of the University of Lincoln), these works changed the face of Lincoln still further. Two new river bridges were built in the city, a 'massive iron swing bridge' at the southern side of Brayford Pool and a wide culvert so that Sincil Dyke could flow beneath the new station. The Great Northern route opened on 17 October 1848, initially between Lincoln and Peterborough *via* Boston, and later on to Gainsborough and routes north on 9 April 1849. Despite early criticism, not without cause ('cramped … inconvenient … much too small') the mock Tudor buildings of the Great Northern station remain an asset to the city.

The two railways had left Lincoln with a lasting and damaging legacy. The High Street now had two level crossings within 100 yards of each other, despite Lincoln Corporation's earlier hopes that a single crossing would be possible, and considerable local opposition in the shape of a petition signed by 219 people. Shunting of wagons over the crossings became a greater issue than the normal passage of trains, and by December 1848 the *Stamford Mercury* reported delays of a quarter of an hour, complaining especially of the Great Northern Railway. The following month was no better, the newspaper being appalled to hear that 'a gentleman was detained at one of the crossings on Monday night for 20 minutes'. Pressure from the Corporation brought about a reduction in frequency by May 1849 but the dual crossings were to plague Lincoln for over a century. The crossings would probably not have been a major inconvenience to Boole personally, living and working north of the city centre at his school in Pottergate, but his staff and any day scholars would certainly have been affected.

George Boole would very probably still have left Lincoln had he reached adulthood before the age of railway travel. With the development of railways, it became more possible to visit the length and breadth of the country, and consequently easier for him to further his career. When he was appointed, in August 1849, as the first professor of Mathematics at the newly-established Queen's College, Cork the relative ease of railway travel meant Boole could be back in his native city when he wished. For example, in December 1849 he returned to Lincoln for Christmas, when a testimonial was presented to him at the *White Hart Hotel*. When responding to the presentation, he made some contrasts between Lincolnshire and the south of Ireland regarding 'railways and public works'. The new Great Southern and Western Railway from Dublin to Cork had in fact just opened in October 1849, to a temporary station outside Cork; the 160 mile journey (very similar to the distance from Lincoln to London) initially took up to eight hours. Boole could have used this new line to reach Dublin and then on to Liverpool or Holyhead by steamer, but his comments about Irish railways suggest he may well have taken a steam packet from Cork's port at Queenstown (now Cobh) direct to London.

THE BUILDING OF THE FIRST LINCOLN CORN EXCHANGE

Beryl George

One of the most iconic buildings in Victorian Lincoln – the first Corn Exchange on Cornhill (now Santander Bank and Waterstones) – was opened the year before George Boole left Lincoln. It took many years, however, from first being proposed to being opened in March 1848. As Boole's pupil, E. L. M. Larken, wrote to his father (George's friend) in December 1847: 'The new Corn Exchange is an improvement which has long been wanted as the merchants and corn factors had before this, no suitable place for meeting…'

A corn exchange was where a corn market was held with grain merchants, millers and maltsters buying directly from farmers. The owner of the corn exchange would gain revenue by hiring 'stands' to corn buyers, and sometimes charging farmers for entry. Since corn markets were only held weekly in most corn exchanges, they were available to be let out for other uses, such as concerts, meetings and dances. This not only increased the income to the exchange owners, but also encouraged the construction of such a building in the first instance.

The first British purpose-built corn exchange opened in Mark Lane, London in 1747, but there were also early commodity markets in Bristol and Liverpool. In 1828 the New Corn Exchange was built in London and a wave of provincial corn exchanges followed including: Norwich (1828), Sheffield (1830), Stowmarket (1836), Bury St Edmunds (1837) and Cambridge (1842).

Cornhill, with market stalls and Corn Exchange. From Rock and Company's Views of Lincoln, 1853. (*Reproduced with permission of Lincolnshire Archives, Lincolnshire County Council. LCL6693*).

There were a number of pressures encouraging the building a corn exchange in Lincoln.

Market days in Lincoln were by all accounts, chaotic. The Corporation ran beast markets, a butcher and butter-market, and these were all regulated to a certain extent. But there was no general market. In 1827, J. W. Drury argued that Lincoln was in great need of one, for

> ...the number of persons who bring commodities for the supply of the city, being obliged to erect their stalls, and range themselves along the sides of the principal street, nearly make up the road...

Although inconvenient, this arrangement was highly lucrative for the High Street shopkeepers, who charged the stall holders (illegal) fees for the privilege of trading in front of their shops. As late as 1846, it was pointed out in the press that this was influencing the discussions of a suitable site for a general market.

In Lincoln, the corn market was held on the Cornhill in all weathers. In July 1838, the *Stamford Mercury* described the scene:

> 'CORN EXCHANGE ... Last Friday, the heavy showers of rain prevented alike farmers selling their grain and merchants from completing their purchases. The Corn-hill was cleared in the lapse of a few moments – just at the very crisis of business; and those who were resolute in finishing a bargain, were driven into the neighbouring public-houses, drapers', saddlers' and shoemakers' shops, or any adjoining shelter. Amongst our merchants the want of a convenient shelter wherein transact their corn business is severely felt; and we believe the time is not far distant when their wish for the erection of a public building will be realised.'

Lincoln also needed a 'great public room'. Boole would have been well aware of this since in 1833, discussions around setting up the Mechanics' Institute, which is considered more fully in a separate chapter, included the suggestion that a 'suite of rooms for concentrating on one spot many public wants of this kind' might be the best solution. This could combine a space for 'a public library, concerts, baths, religious and other public meetings, lectures and exhibitions' with a corn exchange or similar commercial enterprise to make it worthwhile investment.

The first Corn Exchange, Cornhill (now Santander Bank). (*Dave Prichard*).

t was important to keep up with other towns. By the mid-1840s, concern was being expressed that f the problems of the corn market were not resolved, farmers would go elsewhere. With the advent of the railways, the movement of goods was changing rapidly and Lincoln's important river trade was likely to suffer. They simply had to keep up with other towns, or lose trade. As the Town Clerk remarked in October 1844: 'In every place of importance corn-exchanges were now provided, or were being erected ...' Linked to this was civic pride: Lincoln was the county town of an important agricultural county and ought to have an excellent corn exchange.

There was much discussion about where to site the corn exchange. The Corporation was urged to pull down the *City Arms Hotel* and build it in a square next to the Guildhall. Alternatively, they were encouraged to put it on the square (now the site of St Swithin's church), recently vacated as the sheep market. The Cornhill was considered, since it was owned by the Corporation, but this became more plausible with the sale of a large mansion (owned by the Swan family) which formed its eastern side.

The sale took place in November 1844, with the buyers originally intending to open up a road from the east side of the square to Sincil Street, selling and leasing the road frontage for houses and shops. During 1845, discussions in private and public meetings (rumoured or reported in the press), eventually brought the Corporation to the brink of a decision to go ahead with buying the land and building the corn exchange. They then got 'cold feet'. During 1846, local businessmen, especially corn merchants, banded together, first to issue the Council with a 'memorial' (petition) and then setting up the Lincoln Corn Exchange and Market Company.

The provisionally-registered Lincoln Corn Exchange and Market Company issued its prospectus in December 1846. Its intention was:

> in addition to a covered Corn Exchange of ample size and available for many public purposes, to erect other rooms suitable for meetings of public bodies, committees, concerts, lectures, sales of land etc etc.

It was also intended:

> at the sides of and behind the Exchange to erect a stallage market, partially covered, and convenient both for buyers and sellers. The positive certainty of a removal of the stalls from the High-street at no very distant period has induced the Committee to turn their attention particularly to this point.

By February 1847, the Company had come to an agreement with the Corporation to lease the Cornhill and had raised capital of £5000 in 250 shares of £20. In April, an advertisement for tenders for the erection of the exchange appeared, and by June the contract had been awarded to Messrs Kirk and Parry of Sleaford and building commenced straight away.

The Corn Exchange was designed by William Adams Nicholson, the well-known and respected local architect. Nicholson had prepared two different plans for a corn exchange in 1845, when the Corporation was considering it. One was for a single-storey building, the other two-storey, with the exchange hall on the first floor and a vegetable market under it. By 1847, the design had changed significantly, with *The London Daily News* describing the proposed building thus:

> To the back of the present Cornhill, a handsome three-story building, with Corinthian capitals, is to be erected, containing various public rooms; to the rear is the corn exchange, to be lighted from the roof with skylights; this spacious area will afford a site for large public meetings, and there is to be a balcony at one end, the access to which is from the public rooms, which will afford a commodious hustings. In the basement there will be a series of vaults, as well as a large kitchen range of offices. The rest of the site is to be occupied on the south side of the newly laid out street by a covered market, and on the north by an open one.

The foundation stone was laid with great ceremony in September 1847, the new covered market opened in October 1847 and at the end of March 1848, the first corn market was held in the new Corn Exchange, as reported by the *Lincolnshire Chronicle* on 7 April 1848:

> The new exchange was opened last Friday for the sale and purchase of grain. The room is a very excellent one, being spacious, lofty, and well-lighted... The stalls have all been taken, and on Friday there was a large attendance both of buyers and sellers, who spoke in high terms of the value and accommodation of the room.

George Boole no doubt visited the new Corn Exchange on a number of occasions during his remaining time in Lincoln, but the only one recorded in the newspapers was in July 1848, when he is mentioned as being present on the platform for the celebration of the first anniversary of the Penitent Females' Home.

One of the most famous visitors during that period, however, was Prince Albert, who came to Lincoln in April 1849 (by rail) on his way to open the new docks at Grimsby. He was received in the Corn Exchange with great pomp and, once his brief visit had ended, there was a banquet for dignitaries and a ball at the corn exchange. Civic leaders must have felt that the corn exchange was fulfilling its intended function: not only a place of business but suitable for both high ceremony and polite recreation.

LINCOLN'S CHANGING CENTRE 1815-1849

Beryl George

The city of Lincoln in which George Boole grew up was one that was changing in many ways. During his early years, living at 49 Silver Street, next to St Peter at Arches church (no distance from the Stonebow), he would have been acutely aware of the physical developments to roads and buildings around the centre of the lower city during the 1820s. The continued pace of these developments, especially during the 1840s, would also have been of interest.

Lincoln in 1815 was already experiencing some increase in population, with the 1811 census giving the total inhabitants as 8599, up from 7197 in 1801 (although the earlier figure is held to be an underestimate). By 1821 the population had reached 9995 (a 16.2% increase in ten years). After a lower increase by 1831 (12.2%), it grew faster in subsequent decades by 23.9% (1831-41) and 26.2% (1841-51), reaching 17,536 by 1851: an overall increase of 144% on the figure for 1801.

As can be seen from another chapter, there had been some developments in Lincoln by the time of George's birth. The New Road (Lindum Road) – an early bypass – had been completed in 1786, and nearby the newly-built house where George was born was on 'New Street' (Silver Street). Surrounded by recently-built houses and shops, New Street was a good base for John Boole's boot and shoe business (although he probably had better trade when they moved nearer the High Street).

Lincoln High Street, 1819, painted by Augustus Charles Pugin. (*Copyright The Collection: Art and Archaeology in Lincolnshire [Usher Gallery, Lincoln], LCNUG 1927/152*).

But as late as 1827, J. W. Drury, in his *Lincoln and Lincolnshire Cabinet and Annual Intelligencer,* was still able to comment that: 'Lincoln, even in its present state, can only be considered as a ruin: but that ruin is an interesting one'.

Drury came to Lincoln around 1800, and his views of Lincoln in the mid-1820s were written in the light of the changes to the city that he had experienced during those years. He imagined a traveller approaching the city from the south, up the lower High Street, towards the centre:

> The town now improves upon him; he reaches the High-bridge; he beholds the Witham
> with its busy craft on the right, the beautiful Stone-bow (the Guildhall of the city)
> in front, and a number of respectable shops and commodious inns on either hand.
> Through the archway he sees a busy, but rather narrow street running directly up the
> hill, and he finds himself in the centre of bustle, of trade and of business.

Drury also comments that Lincoln is 'not the seat of any fixed manufacture' but 'a place of great trade; and the transit of goods betwixt the Trent and the sea by the way of Boston, fills that part of the city with life and activity'. The economic buoyancy which Drury described in Lincoln was built on the river trade, and much of the development was connected in some way with it.

One of Lincoln's problems was the lack of roads intersecting the High Street. There were plenty of narrow lanes and alleys leading on to it in the lower town, but the increased movement of goods to and from the River Witham and Brayford Pool was becoming hazardous to other road users. One road which was particularly notorious for this was Newland and its continuation westwards to the West Common. In 1824, the Lincoln Turnpike Commissioners decided to widen the road to 60 feet from beyond the racecourse all the way to the Stonebow. This involved taking down a shop on the corner opposite the Stonebow, next to the *Reindeer Inn* (soon to be renamed the *City*

The High Street viewed south from the Stonebow, engraved around 1850. Henry Moss's new premises on the corner of Guildhall Street is on the right, with The Saracen's Head Hotel on the left. (*Reproduced with permission of Lincolnshire Archives, Lincolnshire County Council. LCL26347*).

Arms). The last section of the road was renamed 'Guildhall Street'. Drury approved of 'making the narrow, confined and disagreeable street, a good commodious road', but then he was the Clerk to the Turnpike Trustees.

The 'spirit of improvement' was abroad in Lincoln in the 1820s. In 1827, it was decided to obtain a new Lighting and Paving Act, increasing the powers obtained under the Act of 1791. This was duly passed in May 1828. The Commissioners undertook a valuation of the city, which is a useful source of evidence for buildings standing at that time, and their value. They also regularised street names and had those names displayed. The city was to have gas street lighting for the first time. In practice, despite being hampered by a lack of funds, the Commissioners did carry out a large number of incremental improvements.

During the 1830s, there is less evidence of a desire for improvement. The Municipal Commissioners, visiting Lincoln in 1833, heard that the continued lack of intersecting streets was proving difficult for the siting of premises. One of the frequent demands was for a dedicated market place. Drury suggested that the *Reindeer Inn* could be pulled down, providing an ideal site in front of the Guildhall. This argument was to continue for many years.

By the 1840s, Lincoln was changing at a rapid pace. A new turnpike road was opened running down Canwick Hill, over a re-aligned bridge at St Mary's Street and into the newly-created Melville Street. St Mary's Street (previously Lane), was widened in 1848, with the arrival of the Great Northern Railway Station. This not only created a much-needed side road to the High Street, but also opened up a large area in the form of the station yard.

The building of the Corn Exchange and New Market, examined in another chapter, also brought access through the Cornhill to Sincil Street, thereby increasing trade considerably in that area. In fact the original intention of the buyers of the Swan mansion of the east side of the Cornhill was to create a new street and make money by selling or letting the land for houses and shops.

Guildhall Street and the High Bridge area were also about to change. In June 1847, the Corporation finally sold the *City Arms Hotel* in twelve lots and it was immediately pulled down. One buyer was Henry Moss, who built a large, ornate building on the corner of High Street and Guildhall Street. Apart from his own drapery establishment, there were three 'first-rate shops, with plate glass fronts and excellent houses attached thereto', which he advertised for rent in August 1848. Other parts of the *City Arms'* land became Stephen Harrison's 'Wine Vaults' (on the High Street), and a number of shops were erected on the south side of Guildhall Street by William Rudgard. Writing in 1854, the *Lincolnshire Chronicle* described the consequences of the *City Arms'* sale for Guildhall Street:

that private enterprise has effected a long desired improvement in the street which formerly presented to the view the back walls of a row of stables and an unsightly manure yard. In the place of these eye-sores, a row of handsome buildings for shops has been erected, giving the street a very attractive and pleasing appearance.

The city of Lincoln which George Boole left in 1849 was very different in appearance from the town in which he was born. The High Street was now intersected with paved shopping streets, lit with gas. New shops had been built, others rebuilt or their shop fronts updated. The area between the High Bridge and the Stonebow remained the retail heart of the town, but the opening of the Corn Exchange and New Market was also creating an alternative focus, especially on market days. It had become worthwhile to improve premises and present a modern appearance to the world. Lincoln could not afford to be an 'interesting ruin' any longer.

Antiquaries and Archaeologists in Early Victorian Lincoln

Michael J Jones

In a presentation in 1842 to the recently-founded Lincolnshire Topographical Society, the distinguished local architect, W A Nicholson, reported on the chance discovery during re-development of the south wall of the Roman city in Saltergate. He expressed a regret that he had not been able to make more systematic records of the remains revealed earlier in his career in the city. These were now appearing on an 'almost daily basis' as the pace of development accelerated – and was to increase further with the coming of the railways from 1846.

Nicholson suggested that the Society might accept responsibility for documenting all these discoveries – an innovative idea. In this decade, archaeology, or antiquarianism, was still seen as the preserve of gentleman-scholars, but change was already in the air. There was a greater understanding of stratigraphy, for instance, partly linked to the emergence of the professions, including architecture and geology. A local catalyst for increased awareness had been the Mechanics' Institute founded in 1833 (described elsewhere in this volume by Lesley Clarke). As noted in that article, George Boole and his father were prominent members, and its base, the Greyfriars, was an appropriate one, having been a school. It contained its own museum, a useful receptacle for some local finds. The surveyor and Lincoln mapmaker, J S Padley, was one of those who made donations to its collections. It was to become the City and County Museum in 1906. In the meantime, much of the most important material was claimed by the British Museum.

Several of the Institute's members, led by the architect, antiquarian and Surveyor of Lincoln Castle, Edward James Willson, provided the impetus behind the formation of the Topographical Society. Willson was an acquaintance of Pugin senior (A.W.N. Pugin's father), and he gave the inaugural address, setting out an agenda for its activities. George Boole was another prominent member. Unfortunately, the volume of the Society's Transactions published in 1843 was its only one to appear. Its functions were subsequently assumed by the Architectural and Archaeological Society for Lincolnshire and Nottinghamshire and other successor groups.

Samuel Tuke's depiction of the Roman west gate, as revealed under the castle bank. (*Copyright The Collection: Art and Archaeology in Lincolnshire [Usher Gallery, Lincoln], LCNUG 1927/381*).

Reconstruction of the Roman mosaic pavement found when the County prison within the castle was being extended in 1846. (*Copyright The Collection: Art and Archaeology in Lincolnshire [Usher Gallery, Lincoln]*, HILL/46/4/4/12).

Although discoveries had been made and survival of historic remains noted in previous centuries, it was well into the nineteenth century before accounts were regularly publicised, via local newspapers and other means. Some were considered to be sufficiently significant to be afforded academic articles in national journals. One source of discoveries was the River Witham to the east of the city, which yielded the remarkable Iron Age shield and sword during dredging works in 1826. Among finds reported from the city itself were remains of ancient walls and floors, well-preserved artefacts, and graves and tombs from the many medieval churches and friaries that had formerly existed. Some records of the Roman city wall also noted sculpted architectural fragments and inscribed gravestones that had been re-used in its late Roman rebuilding.

In certain cases, there were unusual reasons for the discoveries – none more graphically than when, in 1836, the landlord of *The Strugglers Inn* on Westgate, Philip Ball, went in search of material to fill up the ditch. He excavated southwards into the castle bank and uncovered the outer arch of the Roman west gate buried within it. It was exposed for only a few days, but fortunately recorded *in situ* before it collapsed forwards and had to be re-buried. A whole saga followed, involving two prison sentences for Philip Ball, but it has to be said that some of his treatment by the authorities was politically motivated: Ball was a radical Liberal, the bench made up almost wholly of Tories.

W.A. Nicholson himself was the architect of the extension to the prison at the castle, which was constructed in 1845-6. Its groundworks encountered the remains of a Roman aristocratic residence containing one of the most impressive mosaic pavements ever found in Lincoln. By this date, the railways were in planning, exposing more remains in the valley. Work for the level crossings on the line of the High Street revealed its Roman predecessor, and one of the chance finds from the construction of Central Station in 1848 was the impressive Viking comb-case with its maker's name *Thorfast* inscribed – in runic letters – to advertise his brand. Collections of pottery from south-west of the city proved to be an early indication of the late Roman pottery industry in the Boultham-Swanpool areas.

uch was the national interest aroused by all these discoveries that Lincoln was selected as the location for only the fifth annual conference (following those at Canterbury, Winchester, York and Norwich) of the recently-founded Archaeological Institute of Great Britain and Ireland. This was a great occasion, in both professional and social terms, lasting more than a week in late July 1848. It welcomed several hundred delegates; some of them, admittedly, attended primarily for the social status and hospitality. Its principal city base was the Assembly Rooms on Bailgate. Among the speakers was the distinguished antiquarian, John Britton. He commented that, 50 years previously, 'archaeology' was not a term in common use, but now it was enthusiastically acknowledged. The outgoing President of the Institute, the Bishop of Norwich, went even further in his welcome:

> Archaeologists were not retracing their steps to carry back humanity to the darker periods of history – they sought to glean from them all that was good, and go forward with a swifter and firmer foot. To those who thought that science tended to encourage ancient superstitions, he would say, the design of archaeology is to cultivate good taste and love of the arts, so that its researches might not only prove an example to stimulate men of the present age, but to serve as a beacon for the guidance of the future.

Even today, field archaeology rarely receives such an articulate endorsement!

The two prominent local architects of the day, Willson and Nicholson, both played major roles in the conference's organising committee, as did several of the local gentry. The content was subdivided into three sections: history, architecture, and antiquities, reflecting the approach of the day. It was an opportunity to synthesise and present the results of research. E. J. Willson was also a prominent speaker, with contributions on the medieval Bishops' Palace, the castle, the 'ancient' Deanery, and St Mary's Conduit. In a brief but profound piece, George Boole discussed a 'philosophical' tract by Bishop Grosseteste. The full proceedings were published in 1850.

The Roman sewer beneath the main Roman street (adjacent to Bailgate). By J.B. Whitwell, based on *The Gentleman's Magazine*, N.S. 38 (July-December 1852).

Members of the Mechanics' Institute were invited to attend the Saturday evening sessions and view the extensive collections of antiquities from the county and beyond that had been created a a temporary museum for the occasion. The published account of these items ran to 30 pages, in addition to the many illustrations. As well as the talks, there were civic receptions. The Mayor o Lincoln made many new friends – if not among those on the Corporation – for his lavish generosity An opportunity to view a stretch of the Roman main sewer uncovered beneath Bailgate a decade or so previously, accessed via the cellar of *The Antelope Inn* (6-10 Bailgate) was one that, sadly, is no longer feasible. As well as the cathedral, the tours included other medieval buildings, including the Greyfriars, and the Roman Mint Wall (as part of a discussion on the 'Ancient Mint'). This last visit was commemorated in a *Punch* magazine article and cartoon, a measure of the national significance of the conference. Other excursions went out of the city and as far as sites in Nottinghamshire, part of the Diocese of Lincoln.

This prestigious event would have lived long in the memory of many influential people, though not necessarily for its academic content. It should have proved a catalyst for greater endeavour in and resources for preserving at least a record of the archaeological remains exposed by development before they were lost for ever, as Nicholson had hoped. The following year, however, the city wall close to the Newport Arch was being demolished, as was the so-called 'John of Gaunt's Palace', a grand late medieval mansion on lower High Street. George Boole was shortly to be on his way to a new life in Cork, while Willson and Nicholson were both to die in the next few years. It would be left to a new generation to assume the mantle on behalf of the city's heritage.

Almost a century after the conference of 1848, and others in 1880 and 1909, the (now 'Royal') Archaeological Institute again held its summer meeting in Lincoln in 1946. That meeting was particularly notable for the unrivalled magisterial survey of Roman Lincoln by the great scholar (Professor Sir) Ian Richmond, based partly on information collected by Tom Baker. Richmond was still able to claim that 'The tale of structures within the [upper] *colonia* is thus a sorry one. All too many opportunities have been missed, as in so many urban sites in Roman Britain'. He was, however, of such academic esteem that he became Adviser to the Lincoln Archaeological Research Committee, newly established by Sir Francis Hill and Baker, and set out its objectives in a research programme for Roman Lincoln. That organisation achieved several of its aims over the next quarter century. Yet it took another generation, and the professionalisation of field archaeology in the 1970s, before the post-Roman remains were afforded the same level of interest, and scientific techniques and a more sophisticated understanding of material evidence began to be more fully developed.

The Lincoln Asylum – innovations in treatment

Nigel Horner and Rob Goemans

This chapter examines the foundation and establishment of the Lincoln Asylum on Union Road, from 1819 onwards, and most tellingly, identifies the connections between George Boole and Dr Edward Parker Charlesworth, one of the key figures in the development of the Asylum as a place of notable innovation and experimentation in new modes of treatment of those defined as insane.

A rector's son from a Nottinghamshire village, Charlesworth was appointed as a physician to the Lincoln County Hospital in 1808, a year after he had graduated from Edinburgh University. He had previously worked with a doctor in Horncastle, Lincolnshire, as part of his studies, had acquired a medical practice in Lincoln and, in 1805, married the daughter of another Horncastle doctor. A veritable polymath with seemingly inexhaustible interests, Charlesworth involved himself in a wide variety of local political affairs. He became the first president of the Lincoln Library in 1814 (which, like the asylum, was funded by subscription), became Mayor's Chamberlain in 1825, joined the City Corporation in 1826, was elected Sheriff in 1827, and unsuccessfully stood for council in 1831 and 1832, before finally giving up his ambition to become Mayor. He was also centrally involved with projects such as a dispensary for the 'sick poor', the hospital library, the development of Dunham Bridge, the River Witham enlargement, the Turnpike Trust, the Board of Health for Cholera, the Lincoln Union, the Mechanics' Institute, and the Lincoln Topographical Society. As the Lincoln historian Francis Hill noted in *Victorian Lincoln*, Charlesworth:

> was able and a hard worker, and the influence which these qualities earned for him was used in a most dictatorial way. Sometimes he drove his associates to feel that it was better to be wrong and against him than right and with him.

In many of these endeavours Charlesworth was supported and accompanied by his friend, the mathematician, Sir Edward Bromhead, mentor to the mathematical physicist George Green, and president of the Lincoln Mechanics' Institute, examined in more detail in Lesley Clarke's chapter. It would have been at the Institute where Charlesworth's and Boole's circles would have crossed most significantly: Boole's father, John Boole, was the curator, and after encountering George, Bromhead supplied the young mathematician for a while with useful mathematics books and journals. George Boole and Bromhead were in regular correspondence with each other on mathematical matters. Bromhead, Charlesworth and his medical colleague, Dr William Cookson, moved in many of the same circles. For example, the 1842 proceedings of the Lincolnshire Topographical Society list Charlesworth as a Vice President and Cookson among the council, alongside George Boole, then aged 27 years. Other members included Sir Edward Bromhead, and Charles Tennyson D'Eyncourt (MP and uncle to Alfred Tennyson). The 1841 census lists Charlesworth as living at number 4

Southern façade of The Lincoln Asylum (now The Lawn). (*Adam O'Meara*).

Pottergate, while George Boole lived at 3 Pottergate, with another Lincoln Asylum doctor, Charles Beattie, living at number 2.

The Lincoln Lunatic Asylum began life in 1803, following a bequest of £100 from a local surgeon, Paul Parnell, for the establishment of such a facility in Lincoln. The cause was taken up by a Committee of Friends to the Establishment of a Lunatic Asylum at Lincoln, the members of which sought to recruit benefactors whose subscriptions would fund the project. Persuading the clergy to support the project in their sermons appeared to be the main strategy deployed. Committee members also made initial decisions relating to the purchase of land, the appointment of an architect, and the setting out of the initial asylum rules. As the project developed, the committee was responsible for appointing staff, approving applications for admission and discharge, and hearing complaints from the director about staff conduct. The committee comprised some of Lincoln's most prominent men including the Lords Yarborough, Brownlow, and Monson, the Bishop and Dean of Lincoln, and three local MPs. Reports of each meeting were sent to the local papers so as to ensure that the benefactors and the public were informed of developments. From October 1810, the committee was also joined by Dr Charlesworth and Dr Cookson, both future surgeons to the asylum. An impressive asylum building designed in the Greek revival style by Richard Ingleman, was opened on Union Road in 1820 at the cost of approximately £15,000.

Whilst the dominant mode of provision for those deemed as mentally unwell had, in the eighteenth century, been private madhouse keepers, an emerging branch of medicine, according to the historian Roy Porter became that of the 'madhouse proprietor'. Yet unlike the 'normal model' of private institutions, run usually by resident proprietors, in closed, discreet, unknown, hidden locations, places to hide away unwanted relatives – the Lincoln Asylum model was different. Funded by public subscription and fund raising, its choice of location, at the heart of historic Lincoln, alongside the Norman castle and cathedral, welcoming visitors and public scrutiny, made it different from the very outset.

By the mid-nineteenth century, the practice of non-restraint was emerging as a watchword, a leitmotif in the progressive treatment of people defined as 'insane'. That such practices were first fully implemented at the Lincoln Asylum from the 1830s is beyond dispute. What remains to be fully understood is why such an innovative 'leap into the dark' occurred in such inauspicious surroundings. As is often the case, a singular tragedy accelerated already developing ideas into a commitment to full implementation. A pauper from the nearby village of Canwick, William Scrivinger, was admitted to the Lincoln Lunatic Asylum on the evening of 22 December 1828. According to the records, Scrivinger 'departed this life about six o'clock this morning, on the 24th December, 1828.' Dr Hewson attended the post mortem examination where 'marks of strangulation' were found on William Scrivinger's neck. It was concluded that he had died of strangulation after being strapped to his bed in a strait waistcoat, which today would be called a strait jacket. Following his death, Dr Charlesworth decided that to prevent this dreadful occurrence from happening again, strait waistcoats were only to be used at night when an attendant was present in the room. There was to be a further full enquiry on 16 February 1829. As a result, the use of the strait waistcoat was discontinued in the institution except under the special written order of the Physician of the Month. It was ordered that an attendant should be present in the room all night whenever it was used. A further development was that a journal of every restraint and control method used would be recorded daily, including the times when it commenced and concluded.

According to the asylum's annual report in 1838, Charlesworth and his colleague, Dr Robert Gardiner Hill, had reduced the incidents of mechanical restraint from 2364, involving 54 patients, in 1830 to just three involving two patients, in 1837.

Lincolnshire-born Dr John Conolly, who as medical superintendent of the Hanwell, Asylum, Middlesex between 1839 and 1844, is often attributed as the architect and founder of non-restraint and moral treatment, readily acknowledged his debt to the Lincoln Asylum and the innovations of Charlesworth and Hill in particular. Conolly stated that the '(i)mprovements and reforms initiated by Charlesworth made Hill's total abolition possible'.

However, all was not harmonious at the Asylum on Union Road. By the time of Boole's departure for Cork in 1849, Charlesworth and Hill had been at loggerheads with each other, with Hill leaving in 1840, though Charlesworth continued to serve as visiting physician until he died in 1853. During the 1840s, mechanical restraint was reintroduced and the radical innovations at the Lincoln Asylum introduced a decade earlier were no longer being applied.

Lincoln contemporaries' appreciation of George Boole

Geoff Tann

It is understandable that John Boole was impressed by his son George's abilities, recounting how at the age of 11 years George had mastered the whole volume of a geometry textbook by John Leslie in a single day. What is more surprising is the frequency of Lincolnshire press reports extolling his abilities and promise during his lifetime, with a crescendo of eulogies after his death. George Boole was clearly recognised and appreciated by Lincoln worthies even before he became Professor at the University of Cork in 1849.

After presenting a lecture on 'The Life and Discoveries of Newton' at the Lincoln Mechanics Institute in February 1835 (where his father was curator), 19-year old George was broadly praised by the Institute's President, Sir Edward Bromhead, who hoped 'that Mr. G. Boole would go on in the course he had commenced, and one day be an honour to Lincoln'. The *Stamford Mercury* on 13 February 1835 described the talk as a 'very able lecture', and George as 'an interesting object' with 'a profound knowledge of the mathematics'. At a meeting of the Lincoln Topographical Society nine years later his paper on 'The planetary system, and the question 'Are the planets inhabited?' was reported in the *Stamford Mercury* as a 'learned paper, replete with profound reasoning'.

The White Hart Hotel, Bailgate, which hosted a farewell dinner to George Boole, in recognition of his professorial appointment at Queen's College, Cork. (*Adam O'Meara*).

National recognition of George's ability arrived in the form of the first gold prize for mathematics from The Royal Society for his paper *On a General Method for Analysis* in 1844. Bromhead presented a published copy to the Lincoln Mechanics' Institute later that year.

A year later George Boole was offered the post of President of the Lincoln Mechanics' Institute but declined, amid allegations reported in the *Lincolnshire Chronicle* on 12 December 1845 that the Institute was degenerating to a Radical club-house. The rector of South Hykeham (and a Minster Yard resident) J. Osmond Dakeyne asserted to the local paper that his appointment 'did it honour. He and his analytical researches obtained the gold medal of the Royal Society and achieved European fame'.

In August 1849 the impending loss to Lincoln following Boole's appointment as Professor of Mathematics in the Royal College at the University of Cork prompted a public meeting at publisher William Brookes' premises. At this gathering, it was resolved that the post would be an 'honour justly due his high talent (which has already attained European reputation), and also to his admirable character, and measure likely to conduce to the success of the Institution with which he will be hereafter connected. That we regret the loss of Mr. Boole from amongst us, and are anxious to show by the presentation of some Testimonial, our esteem for him as a friend, a citizen, and a man'. The meeting's intention was to present Boole with 'some valuable scientific instrument'. Separately, the Lincoln Mechanics' Institute opted to provide a 'framed and glazed address on parchment' at a cost of £5 5s. Money was raised rapidly for the civic testimonial but the presentation had to be delayed until Boole returned to Lincoln at Christmas 1849.

The local press reported the presentation at *The White Hart* of 'a number of very valuable books and a silver inkstand' – in detail across two columns, with speakers noting his 'high moral worth and intellectual capabilities, and their regret that Lincoln was about to lose so distinguished a citizen'. Mayor James Snow described Lincoln-born Boole as:

> held high in the estimation of the whole world as one of the first Mathematicians of the age, and it was to him that the citizens desired to present a testimonial of their esteem for the high character he bore, and for his splendid scientific attainments ...In a mathematical point of view, there could be no doubt that Professor Boole stood high, since he had been called to an important office in a National Institution by the sovereign of his country. They [Lincoln residents] might not, perhaps, be able to appreciate his great talents, but they could feel a degree of pride and pleasure in seeing him so elevated.

Dr Chawner added that 'Mr. Boole was an exemplary citizen, a man of the highest integrity, and I trusted he would long live to enjoy his well-earned reputation'. Mr Whitton wished that 'when Mr Boole had won all glory and renown from his countrymen and the world, he would return among them, and pass the remainder of his days amidst a circle of those friends who had long learned to esteem him'.

At Boole's death, one of the eulogies published in Lincolnshire, in the *Stamford Mercury*, on 2 December 1864, was written by Mr Dyson from Gainsborough, a former fellow staff member at his Doncaster school, who summarised the man:

> There has been no Lincolnshire man since Newton who has attained to a higher position in the realms of thought than George Boole, and no man to whose memory Lincoln could do itself greater honour than in erecting some monument, although, like Newton, no man would care less about it. His most enduring monument is in his works, and in his humble and upright character, the true worth of which was known only to his intimate friends.

The Boole Window, Lincoln Cathedral

Andrew Walker

Shortly after George Boole's untimely death in Ireland on 8 December 1864, a number of his friends and former colleagues met in Lincoln at the city's Guildhall on 11 January 1865 in order to discuss what form of memorial should be created to mark this local man's achievements.

The meeting was chaired by Alderman James Snow, who had attended George Boole's birth. Several of Boole's former pupils were also present, alongside a number of clergy, including the Dean of the Cathedral, the Venerable Archdeacon Kaye, the Rev. E.R. Larken, Rector of Burton, representatives of the city authorities, including Councillor H.K. Hebb, and some of George's longstanding friends such as William and Benjamin Brooke. At the meeting it was decided to form a committee to raise money in order to commission a memorial window in his honour. This was to be situated in Lincoln Cathedral. If resources allowed, an additional memorial was to be constructed elsewhere in the city. Benjamin Brooke acted as Secretary, and Reuben Trotter as Treasurer; and subscription lists to the George Boole Memorial Fund were opened at the different city and county banks.

Despite the significant grief expressed in the city at George Boole's early death, substantial contributions were not immediately forthcoming. In part, this was due to a story in *The Times*, and repeated in many other newspapers, which had suggested that Boole's widow, Mary, and their children had been left in penury. As the *Louth and North Lincolnshire Advertiser* commented on 28 January 1865, if a monument were to be erected in George Boole's memory it should take the form of 'a suitable provision for his helpless widow and orphans'. By 3 February it was reported that these rumours were unfounded and it was made known, according to the *Stamford Mercury*, that a memorial at Lincoln would give 'the greatest satisfaction to the nearest relatives of the lamented professor'. By May 1865, Mary Boole had been granted a civil list pension of £100. According to the published, much-reported citation, this was provided in recognition of her husband's 'distinguished attainments as an original mathematician of the highest order and of his remarkable labours towards the extension of the boundaries of science'. On 16 June, the *Lincolnshire Chronicle* requested that 'now that the Government has granted a pension to Mrs Boole', we trust that 'other gentlemen who have previously hesitated will at once become subscribers to this fund'.

The Boole Window, Lincoln Cathedral. (*Courtesy of the Heslam Trust and Electric Egg*).

The sum of £139 17s. was raised within a few months. However, it was estimated that a further £[...] was required in order to produce a stained glass window of appropriate quality. In order to encourag[e] further donations, a pamphlet was produced, possibly by William Brooke. By August 1865, sufficie[nt] funds had been raised for the George Boole Memorial Fund to select artists to undertake the wor[k] of designing and producing the window. Messrs Ward and Hughes were appointed to take on th[e] task. They were a well-known partnership of stained glass manufacturers. Thomas Ward, with h[is] previous partner, James Nixon, had been responsible for the Cathedral's great east window, installe[d] in 1855, during the tenure as dean of John Giffard Ward – Thomas's brother.

With Henry Hughes as his new partner, following Nixon's death in 1857, Thomas Ward accepte[d] the Boole commission. The window comprised three panels of biblical scenes, with the upper sectio[n] portraying the parable of the talents, the middle part Christ with the doctors in the temple; and th[e] lower scene depicting one of George Boole's favourite bible stories, the calling of Samuel, suggeste[d] by Mary Boole. The three sections were connected by two circular medallions, each with a figur[e] representing study and pious devotion. The memorial window was placed in the nave in August 1866, and finally installed in the north wall of the nave, the fourth from the west entrance, in 1869[.]

Below the window is a plaque with a Latin inscription, reading:

> In memory of George Boole, Doctor of Laws, of Lincoln. A man of acutest intellect and manifold learning, who, being specially exercised in the severer sciences, diligently explored the recesses of mathematics and happily illuminated them by his writings. He was carried off by an untimely death in 1864.

Insufficient funds, though, had been raised by the time of the closure of the memorial appeal to construct any additional monument to George Boole in the city.

Detail of the Boole Window, Lincoln Cathedral. (*Courtesy of the Heslam Trust and Electric Egg*).

The Centenary of his death and the plaque at Pottergate, 1964

Susan Payne

The occasion of the centenary year of George Boole's death was marked in Lincoln by events co-ordinated by three organisations: Lincoln City Libraries, the Mathematical Association (Lincoln Branch) and the Lincolnshire Local History Society (now the Society for Lincolnshire History and Archaeology).

The focus was a day conference and luncheon at the City School, Monk's Road, Lincoln on 7 November. In addition, printed items, manuscripts and *personalia* relating to George Boole were on display at the Central Library in Lincoln from 7 to 21 November.

The day event on 7 November began with the official unveiling of the plaque placed by the Lincoln Civic Trust on the house wall at 3 Pottergate where Boole lived and ran his school from 1840 until 1849 when he took up his post as the Professor of Mathematics at Queen's College, Cork.

The plaque was unveiled by Boole's grandson Sir Geoffrey Taylor (1886-1975), F.S.A. He was the eldest son of Boole's second daughter, Margaret (1858-1935), and the artist, Edward Ingram Taylor (1855-1921).

The day's proceedings continued at the City School with Sir Geoffrey, who had known his grandmother, giving an address on the life of George Boole. Afterwards there was the Centenary Luncheon held in the Lincoln Technical College Refectory attended by a number of local dignitaries. The afternoon session saw Professor T.A.A. Broadbent of the Royal Naval College, Greenwich speaking on 'Boole's Mathematical Work' and R.F. Wheeler of the University of Leicester on 'Boolean Algebra Today'.

Copies of the catalogue of exhibits are at Lincolnshire Archives (LLHS/35/2) and Lincoln Central Library (UP 3703). Items were loaned by academic libraries and members of the Boole family. The Rev. R.H.P. Boole of

George Boole's grandson, Sir Geoffrey Taylor unveiling the commemorative plaque in honour of his grandfather at 3 Pottergate, Lincoln, watched by R. Lucas, 7 November 1964. (*Image courtesy of Lincolnshire Echo and Lincolnshire County Council*).

Grimsby, a great-grandson of George Boole's youngest brother, Charles Boole, lent an origin. portrait of George Boole, a photograph of which is now in the George Boole (Rollett) Collection a Lincolnshire Archives. Gabrielle Boole, a great-grand-daughter of George Boole's younger brothe William John Boole, lent a chart of her family tree, detailing the descendants of Joshua and Bridge Boole. This chart is among the family papers she later gave to Lincolnshire Archives (MISC DON 645).

George Boole plaque at 3 Pottergate. (*Adam O'Meara*).

George Boole: a personal journey to the High Street plaque

Dave Kenyon

Like millions around the world, I first came across Boolean Logic when I was introduced to computer programming; in my case, in the late 1960s. Then again, in 1987 when I had to interrogate the Library of Congress computerised index. This involved using Boolean logical operators (AND, NOT, OR) to search its database over the internet. At this time, I thought Boole must be French, along with mathematicians like LaPlace and Bezier.

In 1993 I started lecturing in digital multimedia. In this field students had to be able to use internet search engines well. This was the time of Altavista, Lycos, Yahoo, and my favourite, EuroFerret. All used algorithms sensitive to Boolean operators, and I tried to teach students to use these effectively.

It was probably about 2010 that a University of Lincoln colleague told me that Boole was not French, but a Lincolnite. Also, he was not just responsible for logical operators, but that his mathematical logic was fundamental to computing and all things digital. I was shocked. How could this be such a secret in Lincoln, the city of his birth?

Using the now imperious Google, I found out as much as I could about Boole and his logic. Among many things, I found out that his first passion was language. By his thirties he could use French, Latin, Greek, German, Hebrew and Italian, all self-taught. He claimed that he turned to

High Street looking south from the Boole plaque. (*Courtesy of the Heslam Trust and Electric Egg*).

mathematics because it was 'cheaper' – the books taking so much longer to understand (especially in their original French or German). This was an important consideration at a time when textbooks were expensive and the Boole family had very limited resources available.

Armed with this knowledge I tried my best to encourage the celebration of Boole in the city via a festival of Arts and Science. In 2012 we managed to host a small celebration called 'BooleFest', which it was hoped would become an annual event by the year of Boole's bicentenary, 2015. Unfortunately, this didn't materialise. However, we launched a virtual tour of Boolean Lincoln on the web, which was developed into a mobile phone application. Also, Boole's association with Lincoln was launched across the world of geocaching, an outdoor activity, in which users employ a global positioning system receiver or mobile device to conceal and find containers, known as 'geocaches', at sites marked by coordinates.

Following BooleFest, I set up the Lincoln Boole Foundation to try to give focus to the Lincoln/Boole connection. We tried recruiting students to an online promotion in conjunction with a website we commissioned from a computing student. By the time this was full of information unearthed about George Boole, it was becoming clear that Cork, the city where he died, was going to eclipse Lincoln in memorialising him.

George Boole plaque on High Street. (*Adam O'Meara*).

My hopes of external funding eventually had to be rethought. However, my work on briefing worthies and producing website content, The Lincoln Boole Tour and BooleFest had made me well versed in things Boolean and able to give public talks. I contacted various bodies across Lincolnshire with a proposal and slowly requests came in. I realised that this was probably the only way funding would be achieved.

By touring Lincolnshire, telling audiences about Boole, the Lincoln Boole Foundation was able to collect just enough money in 2015 for a bicentenary plaque to commemorate Boole as the grandfather of digitality. It was installed on the day of Boole's birth bicentenary, 2 November 2015, some 100 metres from 49 Silver Street, for a long-time his childhood home. On a plinth just north of the High Street and Silver Street junction the plaque states:

> Lincoln man GEORGE BOOLE invented the binary logic at the heart of digital technology. He could be described as, "the man who made the DNA of digitality".

Surrounding the plaque's text is a decorative border made up of 't' and 'f' (True/false); '1' and '0' (binary code) and the international symbols for computing's logic gates.

RECENT MEMORIALS TO GEORGE BOOLE IN LINCOLN

Andrew Walker

In recent years, a variety of memorials to George Boole, both permanent and temporary, have been created in the city to accompany the stained glass window dedicated to him and the two plaques in his honour at 3 Pottergate and the High Street.

Boole is amongst the 'city greats' commemorated on a plaque on an obelisk, which since 1996 has been situated at St Mark's, but that previously had been located on High Bridge from 1760 until 1939. Here, Boole is remembered amongst a number of other Lincoln luminaries. Boole has also been remembered on one of the City of Lincoln interpretation boards, located on the north-west side of the junction of Eastgate, Northgate and Pottergate.

During the bicentenary of Boole's birth, in 2015, in addition to the plaque unveiled on the High Street, (and examined in Dave Kenyon's chapter), a number of other commemorative activities and structures marked the occasion. A digital arts festival was held at the University of Lincoln – the 'Frequency Festival of Digital Culture' – a collaboration between Threshold Studios and

A sculpture entitled 'Perhaps (An Investigation Outside the Laws of Thought)' by Raqs Media Collective, displayed on the south bank of the Brayford Pool in Summer 2016. The work was inspired by George Boole. (*Lesley Clarke*).

Mock-up of George Boole sculpture *in situ* outside Lincoln Central Railway Station. (*Courtesy of the Heslam Trust and Electric Egg*).

the University of Lincoln. It included the screening of a special film in honour of George Boole, narrated by Jeremy Irons. An exhibition was also staged at the University of Lincoln between July and September of that year, located in the Great Central Warehouse Library. The exhibition was curated by the University College, Cork and was on display in Cork simultaneously.

Since the bicentenary of George Boole's birth further actions have been taken to mark the links of George Boole to Lincoln, the city that played such a formative part in his development. In 2016, a temporary artwork was situated on the south bank of Brayford Pool, near to the University's Minerva Building. The sculpture, entitled 'Perhaps (An Investigation Outside the Laws of Thought)', comprised two interlocking arcs, which reflected the surrounding water and foliage. This was created by internationally-acclaimed Raqs Media Collective, based in New Delhi.

The Boole Technology Centre (BTC), built at a cost of £6.8 million, was opened in February 2017, as a major building on Lincoln's Science and Innovation Park, situated off Beevor Street. The Park was founded by Lincolnshire Co-op and the University of Lincoln in 2012 on part of the historic former Ruston Bucyrus engineering site. The BTC itself retains part of the Ruston Bucyrus substation within its design in homage to Lincoln's industrial past. The Centre offers a hub for private sector investment and innovation alongside contemporary academic research science facilities in the centre of Lincoln. At the entrance to the building, a plaque honours George Boole, referring to him as the 'grandfather of the digital age'.

Elsewhere in the city, a new residential road has been named in recognition of Boole. Situated on the site of the former Moorland Infant and Nursery School, which closed in 2012, George Boole Drive is home to a £7.75 million residential estate, opened in 2019, comprising 14 shared ownership

George Boole Drive. (*Dave Prichard*)

houses and 46 rental properties offered at an affordable rate by the City of Lincoln Council.

A permanent sculpture dedicated to George Boole has also been produced for the city following the bicentennial of his birth in 2015. Since 1963, the Heslam Trust has been purchasing or contributing to the purchase of art for the city of Lincoln and its inhabitants. This has included in recent years 'Empowerment', a sculpture by Stephen Broadbent, a 16-metre tall sculpture located across the River Witham, next to the Waterside Shopping Centre, which was installed in 2002 and, for the cathedral, a sculpture by Aidan Turner, entitled 'Our Lady of Lincoln'. The Trust was instituted by James Heslam (1893-1965), who had various business interests across the county. In connection with George Boole, the current trustees of the Heslam Trust have declared: 'we feel the city of Lincoln should acknowledge that this important man was born here in Lincoln and be remembered with pride'. Peter Manton, who chairs The Heslam Trust, stated that:

> It is clear that George Boole and James Heslam had something in common – their dedication to their communities – and the Trustees are sure that a commemorative work to celebrate George Boole would have been happily approved by James Heslam.

Following its decision to commemorate Boole, the Trust commissioned the internationally-regarded sculptor and portrait painter Antony Dufort to produce a bronze artwork of George Boole that was to be prominently displayed in the city centre, possibly within the Transport Hub, near to the former Great Northern Railway station.

Antony Dufort's previous public works of art include an ornamental bronze of Her Majesty the Queen in Armoury House, London, a sculpture of Margaret Thatcher for the Members' Lobby in the House of Commons, Westminster and several sculptures of miners – one at the National Coalmining Museum in Wakefield, and another, a miner testing for gas, produced for Nottinghamshire County Council. Dufort has also designed a £2 coin for the Royal Mint, bearing the image of Britannia, which was issued in 2015.

our designs for a sculpture of George Boole were the subject of a public vote during 2017, of which three were produced by Antony Dufort and a fourth by Martin Jennings. The chosen design by Antony Dufort – a bronze sculpture on a scale 25% above life size – depicts George Boole in front of a blackboard, accompanied by an attentive boy and girl, each holding slates. Boole is represented teaching the basics of Boolean logic. Whilst working at Hall's Academy, which is examined in Rob Wheeler's earlier chapter in this volume, Boole's prospectus advertised 'arithmetical and mathematical sciences taught by the blackboard', a pioneering teaching technique at the time. The sculpture also represents Boole holding a copy of his book, *The Laws of Thought*, with an extract from that text displayed on the blackboard.

Kate Ellis, Strategic Director for Major Developments at City of Lincoln Council, noted at the time of the launch of the public vote in February 2017 that:

> George Boole has played a vital role in the advancement of computer science. It's incredible to think every time we use a smart phone or a computer, it is the work of a Lincoln man nearly two centuries ago that made it possible. We are excited to see a new sculpture celebrating Boole's work and hope to find a suitable, central location for it within the new transport hub development.

It is pleasing to see that the significance of George Boole, and indeed the city's influence upon his development, is now being widely acknowledged in Lincoln itself.

The Boole Technology Centre, Lincoln Science and Innovation Park, Beevor Street. (*Dave Prichard*).

The George Boole (Rollett) Collection

Susan Payne

Letters from George Boole (1815-1864), F.R.S., mathematician and logician, are to be found spread across a number of libraries in the United Kingdom since he wrote prolifically to friends and professional associates and, as he was known to be a ground-breaking mathematician in his own lifetime, they were often carefully retained by the recipients. Letters and notes kept by George Boole himself, however, continued to be held by the family for years after his death. They were later dispersed and it is only now, following the donation to Lincolnshire Archives of a collection previously in private custody, that his surviving papers as a whole can be appreciated.

The gift of the George Boole (Rollett) Collection (BRC) to Lincolnshire Archives in 2015 is also significant since it offers an important resource in the city of Lincoln where Boole was born, lived and worked until 1849 when he became the founder Professor of Mathematics at Queen's College, Cork. Generous funding for cataloguing this collection has been provided by the University of Lincoln and, therefore, letters written from and to George Boole and other sources which further illuminate his life in Lincoln are now publicly available for the first time.

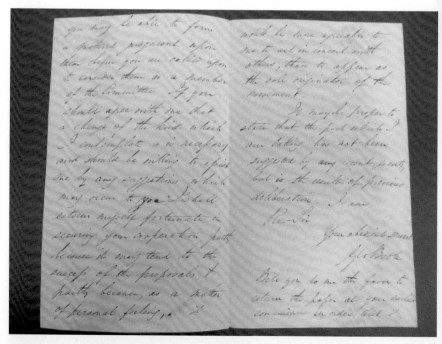

Extract from letter of George Boole to the Rev. Edmund R. Larken, 12 August 1847. (*George Boole [Rollett] Collection, Lincolnshire Archives, Lincolnshire County Council*).

George Boole's unexpected death in 1864, while still in post at Queen's College, saw his widow, Mary Boole, move to London with their five daughters, aged from six months to eight years. In 1874, she gave his unpublished mathematical papers to The Royal Society, London, but fearful of private matters entering the public domain, she held on to the letters, other miscellaneous notes, the reminiscences and returned letters which she had received herself from several of his personal and professional friends.

By the time of Mary Boole's death in 1916, if not before, the papers were dispersed to her three oldest daughters or their children: Mary Ellen Hinton (1856-1908), Margaret Taylor (1858-1935), and Alice Stott (1860-1940). Lincolnshire Archives now holds the items once kept by Alice Stott and a few items which were previously held by Margaret Taylor's son, Sir Geoffrey I. Taylor (1886-1975), FSA, the renowned physicist and mathematician. Surviving letters and other items kept by Mary Ellen Hinton or her sons (including letters and notes of George Boole's sister, Mary Ann Boole) have been acquired by University College (previously Queen's College), Cork. Some items, including printed and photocopied material, were passed to University College, Cork and Lincoln Central Library by the executors of Sir Geoffrey I. Taylor. The Royal Irish Academy in Dublin also holds some papers from his executors.

The BRC comprises both personal papers of George Boole and also biographical research materials amassed from the late 1960s until the 1980s, first by Arthur P. Rollett (1902-1968) and then by his son, Dr John M. Rollett (1931-2015). Arthur P. Rollett was born in Lincolnshire and was a mathematics teacher and Inspector of Schools before his retirement in 1965, when he decided to write the first major biography of George Boole. He undertook an extensive amount of detailed research which was enthusiastically supported by academics and Boole's descendants. Sadly, he died before completing the work. John M. Rollett continued to undertake research, but was unable to bring the biography to publication. In the meantime, Boole's letters were made available to researchers, but eventually, as it was always intended, Rollett transferred them to Lincolnshire Archives before he died.

The custodial history of the original papers in the BRC is documented in the collection. It is the story of their transfer from academic to academic intent on writing about the work of George Boole. Alice Stott and her husband, Walter, were active in mathematical circles with Alice becoming President of the Liverpool Mathematics Society. In 1889 Alice evidently borrowed for study the manuscript mathematical papers of her father from the Royal Society. She returned them in 1896, but, in the meantime, she allowed them to be transcribed and typescript copies made. One of the three copies produced is in the BRC. In 1916 Alice and Walter Stott sent Boole's letters along with the typescripts to Philip E. B. Jourdain (1879-1919), an historian of mathematics and logic, to assist him in his works on Boole's writings.

After Jourdain's death in 1919, the papers passed to his literary executor, the philosopher, Arch[...] E. Heath (1887-1961). Heath's widow later gave them to his colleague, Rush Rhees (1904-198[...] It was Rhees who eventually sent them, in 1965 and 1966, to Arthur P. Rollett, knowing of h[...] research for Boole's biography.

A few items were sent to Arthur P. Rollett from Sir Geoffrey Taylor. These include a notebook wit[...] 'George Boole Lincoln' in Boole's handwriting on the inside cover. It appears to have been original[...] used to record passages or his thoughts relating to the writings of the theologian and philosophe[...] Bishop Joseph Butler (1692-1752) and afterwards used to note down useful words and phrases i[...] German. It is interesting that the typed transcripts of papers at The Royal Society include five page[...] of 'Bishop Butler's Sermons'. In a letter to Rollett, Sir Geoffrey Taylor stated that he thought he ha[...] received the notebook from his aunt, Alice Stott, at her death in 1940.

Summary

The Rollett Collection comprises the following:

Letters from or to George Boole, 1839-1864:

> Correspondents include personal friends and professional associates, with most letters from or to: William Brooke, Charles Doughty, Robert Leslie Ellis, Duncan F. Gregory, T.A. Hirst, Robert A Jamieson, the Revd Edmund R. Larken, T.W. Moffet, Francis W. Newman, John Penrose senior, John Penrose junior, Francis Cranmer Penrose, Isaac Todhunter.

Notebook kept by George Boole in Lincoln.

Obituaries of George Boole collected by his sister, Mary Ann Boole.

Letters and reminiscences sent to Mary Boole, his widow:

Thomas Dyson, Robert A. Jamison, T.W. Moffet, the Revd Edmund R. Larken.

Reminiscences sent by Thomas Dyson to George Boole's sister, Mary Ann Boole.

Typed transcripts (made 1889-1896) of George Boole's papers at the Royal Society, London.

Papers and works by George Boole (printed):

Mathematical Analysis of Logic, 1847; *On the Philosophical Remains of Bishop Grosseteste*, 1848; *The Right Use of Leisure*, 1848; *The Claims of Science*, 1851; *The Social Aspect of Intellectual Culture*, 1855; a bound volume of Boole's published papers.

Research materials of Arthur P. Rollett and Dr John M. Rollett:

Correspondence: relating to the custodial history of the BRC, with libraries and individuals relating to source material, with descendants of George Boole, photographic copies of Boole family photographs, contemporary photograph of Thomas Dyson, transcripts of original letters and papers in the BRC, draft chapters of *George Boole F.R.S.* by Arthur P. Rollett, photocopies of letters held in other libraries, Boole family history research, research notebooks and other research materials.

Access

The cataloguing of the BRC is in its final stages and not yet available online. Please contact Lincolnshire Archives for updated information and advice about using the public search room: Lincolnshire Archives, St Rumbold Street, Lincoln, LN2 5AB, tel: 01522 782040, enquiries: lincolnshire.archives@lincolnshire.gov.uk

Suggestions for further reading:

ARCHIVAL COLLECTIONS:
George Boole (Rollett) Collection at Lincolnshire Archives, St Rumbold Street, Lincoln.

PRIMARY SOURCES:
Lincolnshire Chronicle. Stamford Mercury. Kelly's *Directories of Lincolnshire.* White's *Directories of Lincolnshire.*

SECONDARY SOURCES:
Birch, Neville, 'The Archaeologians visit Lincoln', in Sturman, Christopher, ed., *Lincolnshire People and Places*, Society for Lincolnshire History and Archaeology, Lincoln, 1996.

Brook, Shirley, Walker, Andrew and Wheeler, Rob, eds, *Lincoln Connections: Aspects of City and County Since 1700*, Society for Lincolnshire History and Archaeology, Lincoln, 2011.

City of Lincoln Council, Lincoln Heritage Database.

Grattan-Guinness, I., 'George Boole', in *Oxford Dictionary of National Biography*, 2004.

Hill, Francis, *Georgian Lincoln*, Cambridge University Press, Cambridge, 1966.

Hill, Francis, *Victorian Lincoln*, Cambridge University Press, Cambridge, 1974.

Hodson, Maurice, *Lincoln Then and Now, Volumes I-III*, North Hykeham, 1982-87.

Jones, M. J., *Roman Lincoln: Conquest, Colony and Capital. Revised Edition*, Stroud, 2011.

MacHale, Desmond, *The Life and Work of George Boole: A Prelude to the Digital Age*. Second Edition, Cork University Press, Cork, 2014.

MacHale, Desmond and Cohen, Yvonne, *New Light on George Boole*, Cork University Press, Cork, 2018.

Mills, Dennis and Wheeler, Robert C. eds, *Historic Town Plans of Lincoln, 1610-1920*, published for the Lincoln Record Society and The Survey of Lincoln by Boydell and Brewer, Woodbridge, 2004.

Roberts, Stephen, *Lincoln in 1837*, Kindle Direct Publishing, Birmingham, 2019.

Stocker, David. ed., *The City By The Pool*, Oxbow Books, Oxford, 2003.

Related chapters in Survey of Lincoln's *Neighbourhood Booklet* series:
Herridge, John and Jones, Michael J., 'The Lawn', in Walker, A., ed., *Uphill Lincoln I: Burton Road, Newport and the Ermine Estate*, 2009, pp. 15-17.

Mills, Dennis and Thorpe, Victoria, 'Servant-keeping households in the Minster Close, 1841', in Walker, A., ed., *Lincoln's Castle, Bail and Close*, 2015, 51-53.

Tinley, Ruth, 'Lincoln Corn Exchange', in Walker, A., ed., *Lincoln's City Centre South of the River Witham*, 2016, pp. 36-38.

Walker, Andrew, 'Carline Road', in Walker, A., ed., *Uphill Lincoln I:Burton Road, Newport and the Ermine Estate*, 2009, pp. 55-57.

Ward, Arthur, 'Places of worship in the neighbourhood', in Walker, A., ed., *Lincoln's City Centre: North of the River Witham*, 2015, pp. 18-23.

WEBSITES:
https://arcade.lincoln.gov.uk
www.heritageconnectlincoln.com
www.lincoln-record-society.org.uk
www.lincstothepast.com
www.slha.org.uk